100 GREATEST™ WOMEN ON COINS

Ron Guth

Foreword by Charmy Harker

Whitman Publishing, LLC
PUBLISHING SINCE 1934
www.whitman.com

Whitman Publishing, LLC
Atlanta, GA

100 Greatest Women on Coins

Whitman Publishing, LLC
PUBLISHING SINCE 1934
www.whitman.com

3101 Clairmont Road • Suite C • Atlanta GA 30329

Correspondence concerning this book may be directed to the publisher,
Attn: 100 Greatest Women on Coins, at the address above.

ISBN: 0794843360
Printed in China

Disclaimer: No warranty or representation of any kind is made concerning the accuracy or completeness of the information presented, or its usefulness in numismatic purchases or sales. The opinions of others may vary. The author may buy, sell, and sometimes hold certain of the items discussed in this book.

Caveat: The price estimates given are subject to variation and differences of opinion. Some coins trade infrequently, and an estimate or past auction price may have little relevance to future transactions. Before making decisions to buy or sell, consult the most current available information. Grading of coins is subject to wide interpretation, and opinions can differ. Past performance of any item in the market is not necessarily an indication of future performance, as the future is unknown.

Contents

An Indian Head cent, 1864, showing Miss Liberty wearing a Native American headdress.

Miss Liberty in a 1919 patriotic poster, and on a U.S. silver half dollar of the era.

I am *extremely* honored to be given the opportunity to write the foreword for Ron Guth's wonderful book about the 100 Greatest Women on Coins. There are many fascinating women who have been depicted on coins throughout the world, many more than most people would have imagined. From historical women like Cleopatra to modern women like Princess Diana, this book is a fascinating look into the contributions and sacrifices that made these women worthy of being depicted on coinage.

I was in my late 30s before I was introduced to the numismatic world when I inherited several boxes of U.S. coins from my aunt. Before that, I had no clue what a numismatist was. Included among these coins was an old metal box full of pennies that had a portrait of an Indian on the front. I had never seen an Indian Head cent before—I just assumed Abraham Lincoln had always been on the U.S. cent—and was quite intrigued by the beauty and design of the Indian on these pennies.

That inspired me to learn all I could about Indian Head cents, and the more I learned, the more I fell in love with them. I later discovered that, even though some historians felt that James Longacre's image on the Indian Head cent was inspired by his young daughter Sarah, the portrait of the "Indian" was actually a personification of Lady Liberty. Not only is Lady Liberty one of the most widely used images on U.S. coinage, she is the 11th most popular woman in Ron's book.

I eventually became a dealer in all things pennies. At first, I hadn't paid attention that the coin industry was so male dominated, not that it would have mattered. To me, it was all about the coins, but I soon realized that being one of only a handful of female dealers meant I would have to work a lot harder to prove myself to gain the trust of my male peers. In order to continue learning about coins and becoming more knowledgeable, I joined several specialty coin clubs, including Women In Numismatics. I am now very proud to be WIN's president.

When Ron approached me about possibly having the members of WIN assist him in choosing their 100 favorite women on coins, including narrowing down the top 20 of that 100, I was once again delighted and intrigued. Having a book about women on coins will definitely help highlight the important role women have played throughout history. It might also inspire more women to become interested in numismatics. As for me personally, I hadn't imagined there could be enough women depicted on coins to fill a book. Not only was I wrong, I was pleased to learn that so many women, both actual and allegorical, throughout history were greatly revered and given such a high honor by having their images featured on coins.

We see in Ron's book that women are regularly shown on coins throughout the world and many of those international coins are found in general circulation. Five of the American women in the top 20 are depicted in the First Spouse series, but those coins are minted mainly for collectors. In the top 20, there are only three other American women on U.S. coins that are readily found in the change in your pocket. I hope that Ron's book will create a spark of interest that will put more women on regular circulating U.S. coins—perhaps even the penny!

It is quite evident that Ron Guth has done an extensive amount of meticulous research into the history of women who have appeared on coins, and he describes these great women in such a way that makes it easy to understand what made them so special as to be honored with their image carved into a coin. *100 Greatest Women on Coins* is a fascinating look into the important role women have played throughout numismatic history and throughout history in general.

Charmy Harker—*The Penny Lady*®
Irvine, California

Charmy Harker acquired her passion for coins late in life after inheriting a group of coins from an aunt. Since she was busy raising a family and working fulltime as a litigation paralegal, she felt she didn't have enough time to learn about all the coins she had acquired. Having always enjoyed Native American history, she decided to narrow down her studies, learning about and specializing in Indian Head cents. She began upgrading the Indian Head cents she had inherited, then selling off the duplicates to help pay for new acquisitions. She soon did the same thing with Lincoln cents and early copper coins, and eventually turned her passion into a fulltime business. Today popularly known as The Penny Lady, Charmy travels all over the country buying and selling high-quality coins at most of the major shows, as well as through her Web site, www.thepennylady.com. She belongs to many hobby organizations, has won numerous awards for competitive exhibiting of her collections, and frequently writes online about numismatic topics.

Miss Liberty, as seen on a variety of U.S. coins.

Above: Charmy Harker in action as a coin dealer and researcher.

This book is a celebration of the hundreds of women who have appeared on coins from ancient times to the present. This is a book about mothers, daughters, sisters, wives, empresses, queens, ballerinas, athletes, goddesses, regents, allegorical figures, and the many forms in which women have appeared on coins. It's the story of women who have made important contributions to history, politics, the arts, the sciences, and myriad other fields. In many cases, their stories are familiar to most readers; in others, they will be new.

The inspiration for this book was a young lady named Alice Paul.

I first "met" Alice in 2012 when she appeared on the First Spouse gold coin issued in conjunction with Chester Alan Arthur's Presidential dollar. Chester Arthur was a widower while president, thus he had no First Lady, and an appropriate substitute was required for the First Spouse coin issued for his presidency. This situation was not without precedent. For example, Thomas Jefferson's First Spouse coin features the same Draped Bust design that appeared on many of the regular coins issued during his term in office. The Presidential $1 Coin Act of 2005 (the authorizing legislation for the First Spouse coins) stated simply:

"In the case of any President who served without a spouse — (i) the image on the obverse of the bullion coin corresponding to the $1 coin relating to such President shall be an image emblematic of the concept of 'Liberty' — (I) as represented on a United States coin issued during the period of service of such President; or (II) as represented, in the case of President Chester Alan Arthur, by a design incorporating the name and likeness of Alice Paul...."

But, who was Alice Paul? How was she connected to President Arthur? Was she a girlfriend? A relative? Was she an important public figure during his term? Her name was unfamiliar and I suspect that few people knew who she was when she burst onto the numismatic scene in 2012.

Alice Paul was a significant figure during the early part of the 20th century when women struggled for the right to vote. She was a feminist of the most radical sort—the kind who chained herself to the fence outside the White House or who went on a hunger strike while in prison. She, as much as any other suffragist, deserves thanks for American women's ability to vote today.

However, Alice's connection to Chester Arthur was tenuous, at best. They never knew each other personally because she was only three years old when Arthur died. Rather, this was an opportunity for the Congress and the secretary of the Treasury of our time, despite the weak connection, to showcase one of America's great feminists—one whose appearance on millions of coins would provoke curiosity and investigation.

Ironically, I met Alice again shortly thereafter and I got to know her very well.

In early 2013 I took an online course at the American Public University titled "The History of American Women," which examined the contributions women made to the building of America from the Colonial period through the fight against slavery, the struggle for the right to vote, the Progressive movement, the Equal Rights Amendment, and similar struggles. My professor, Dr. Loni Bramson, taught about women whose stories had gone untold, intentionally or unintentionally. Alice Paul, of course, was an important player in American history.

The course made me wonder about women on coins; more specifically, how many different women have appeared on coins? "How interesting," I thought, "would it be to compile a list of all the women who have appeared on coins?" This would give collectors a checklist of women from which to build a comprehensive collection.

The Methodology of Selecting the 100 Greatest Women

The first step in developing this list was to survey all the coins from ancient times to the present for images of women. The goal was not to identify every single coin that bore a portrait of a woman (that would be a huge undertaking), but to identify as many different women as possible. Only coins with monetary value were considered because they were most likely to be seen by the general public; pattern coins, medals, and tokens were not included in the results because they fall into the realm of collector coins or exonumia and the public is generally unfamiliar with them. However, medals, pattern coins, and tokens have been used as auxiliary illustrations throughout this book, and in cases where coins are unavailable I have recommended them as collectible alternatives.

The Internet became the starting point for the survey. The first stop was the Wildwinds Web site (www.wildwinds.com), which contains a plethora of information about ancient Greek, Roman, Byzantine, Celtic, and English coins. For Greek coins, the Wildwinds site is organized by issuing authorities; Roman coins are in both chronological and alphabetical order; Byzantine coins are in chronological order; Celtic coins are ordered by tribe or region; and English coins appear in chronological order. The Wildwinds site is an important resource for anyone collecting or interested in ancient coins.

For modern coins, I consulted the *Standard Catalog of World Coins* (SCWC) by Krause Publications. Each SCWC volume covers a complete century, starting with 1600. These are large books reminiscent of telephone books (remember them?) from large cities, and I literally went through each of the hundreds of pages scanning for images of women. Unfortunately, not every coin type is illustrated in the *Standard Catalog*s, requiring a reading of almost every entry. Next, I consulted my library of books on German coins; then it was back to the Internet to search eBay and other online venues for coins with images of women.

Initially, I hoped to find as many as 200 different women on coins. It was easy to identify the usual suspects: Queen Elizabeth II, Catherine the Great, Queen Victoria, Maria Theresa, and all the American interpretations of Miss Liberty (seated, standing, and otherwise). The list grew quickly to more than 200 different women, then 300, then 400, and finally slowed down once 500 women were identified. By the time the survey was completed, I had identified more than 600 different women who had appeared on coins throughout history. (The complete list appears at the back of this book.)

An analysis of the list revealed four distinct categories: real (or actual) women; goddesses; allegorical women, who represent an idea, concept, or nationality; and women in art (for example, the Mona Lisa). Real (or actual) women were usually nation- or empire-specific while broader themes such as sports, dance, and science often appear on the coins of multiple countries.

Whittling down the list to the 100 Greatest Women on Coins required outside help. I contacted my good friend Charmy Harker (aka The Penny Lady), who was the president of Women in Numismatics (WIN), and asked her if she might solicit the members of her organization to vote on the 100 Greatest. She asked me to present a proposal at the annual WIN membership meeting at the American Numismatic Association World's Fair of Money in August 2014, where it was approved enthusiastically. Charmy sent the master list of names to the WIN membership via email and regular mail. Eighteen respondents (out of approximately 140 members) chose the women you will read about here. I had hoped to say that this was a book about women selected by women, but WIN has some male members and I thought it impolite to deny their participation since they are legitimate members of the organization.

Respondents were asked to select 100 women and rank them in order of importance or interest, with 1 being the most significant and 100 being the least. Most respondents chose a full roster of 100 women; some selected only the top 20; others omitted a name or two. A few write-in votes were cast for women I missed in the original survey.

In tabulating the results, the top 20 women were assigned a weighted value. The highest-ranked woman received 20 points; the second-highest received 19 votes; and so on. The 21st through 100th women received half a point each. While the voting represented a popularity contest of sorts, the weighting of the votes placed special emphasis on the women who appeared most frequently in the top 20, but it also gave every woman a chance to make it into the 100 Greatest.

Two mistakes on my part necessitated adjustments to the voting results. Queen Elizabeth II appeared on the ballot twice: as Queen Elizabeth and Elizabeth II. Mary (the mother of Jesus) appeared as: Madonna; Madonna and Child; Mary and Joseph; and "Our Lady of...." I combined their respective entries and, to prevent over-voting, I only included the highest-ranked vote by any respondent. This adjustment lowered their respective weighted scores. However, even with the adjustment, Mary's no. 1 rank remained the same and Queen Elizabeth II's ranking dropped one or two levels. No woman gained entry to the 100 Greatest because of this adjustment, nor did any get kicked out. Also, Athena and Minerva both appeared in the top 100 (Athena as no. 27 and Minerva as no. 97). Since they are both the same goddess, their votes were combined, Minerva was eliminated, and Vesta moved into 100th position.

A casual analysis of the voting reveals that respondents preferred real women, were U.S.-centric, and had a religious bent. I suspect that the rankings in future editions will be affected by the addition of new women, expansion of the voting base to include more and different members, and publicity regarding a particular woman.

How Do Women Get on Coins?

This question "How do women get on coins?" comes up quite frequently along with its companion question, "How can we get more women on coins?" The answer to the first question can be found in the historical record by examining the context in which women appeared on coins.

The first coins appeared in Lydia (part of modern-day Turkey). The invention of coins supplanted the old barter system in which goods were traded between buyers and sellers. As a result, their use spread rapidly throughout the ancient world. The ancient Greeks and Romans favored gods and goddesses on their coins; portraits of actual individuals were a later invention. Some of the earliest depictions of women on coins were of nymphs romping with satyrs, the goddess Nike, the Gorgon Medusa, Aphrodite, and others. Gods and goddesses were such an important part of the lives of the Greeks and Romans that choosing them was natural if not expected. Though the historical record is inexact, we can assume that all of the images were chosen by men. In the Roman Republic, we know who chose the images on coins because the moneyers (who were male) actually signed their coins. In Imperial Rome, men dominated the portraiture on coins and women only appeared because of their relationship to the ruler (sister, mother, daughter, etc.). The choice of a woman could be for political purposes during their lifetime or posthumous to memorialize or deify them. Women rarely controlled the portraiture on coins of the ancient world except in instances where they ruled or controlled power (Cleopatra VII of Egypt and powerful women such as Julia Domna and Julia Maesa are examples).

As Christianity rose, images on coins became more religious and less secular, and portraiture was dominated by Christ and male rulers. In the Muslim world, women rarely appeared on coins, but portraiture was generally scarce anyway, though men had a slight advantage as rulers. As the European nations emerged, so did women's portraiture as queens, abbesses, and wives. This trend continued until the late 20th century, when a curious trend emerged.

In the past few decades, nations and mints discovered a lucrative trade in commemorative coins. To compete for the attention of collectors and their money, mints have scoured literature, art, science, the bottom of the barrel, and you-name-it for popular subjects to place on their coins and stimulate sales. Female subjects have proven to be particularly popular, which is why we now have coins featuring Marilyn Monroe, Cinderella, and Malvina, the Fairy with the Turquoise Hair. Never in the history of coins has there been such a burst of female subjects in such a short period of time.

Thus, the answer to "How do women get on coins?" has changed over time. Historically, to merit a portrait on a coin, the woman had to be related to an important male or in charge herself. In recent decades, women are chosen for their popularity, their star power, or their ability to sell coins.

Similarly, the answer to "How can we get more women on coins?" has changed. In the old days, we, as individuals, had no chance of influencing the decision to place a woman's image on a coin. Today, however, it is possible for any of us to directly petition a mint with a suggestion for placing a woman's image on a coin.

The Format of This Book

Each of the 100 Greatest Women on Coins is represented in this book by: one or more images; a historical essay; descriptions of the coin or coins on which she appears; interesting facts; and estimates of the degree of difficulty that collectors will encounter when attempting to collect a particular woman on a coin. The first 10 women, because of their importance and higher ranking, received a lengthier narrative and more images than the last 90, though it should be repeated that the ranking of a woman in this book has more to do with her popularity among the people who voted for her than for the woman's actual historical significance.

Images. In every case, an attempt was made to obtain the highest-quality image possible. Nonetheless, image quality varies depending on the source. Coins were selected that had the greatest visual impact or interest. Some women, such as Helen Keller, Elena Aladova, and Ingrid Bergman, appear on only a single coin, thus there were no other options. Other women, such as Queen Elizabeth II, Queen Victoria, and the Virgin Mary, appear on hundreds of different coins in a variety of design types, or they appear on the coins of several countries, leading to an abundance of choices for images. For most women, it was a pleasant matter of selecting from several images. In cases of extreme rarity, the best images came from numismatic auction houses, which seem to be one of the preferred venues for coins of the highest condition or the greatest rarity. This was especially true of the coins of ancient times, which are generally not available in your local coin store or which tend to be in deplorable condition. The author purchased many coins for this book simply to have them photographed. This resulted in a level of image quality that is available nowhere else. It also gave the author a real sense of what the readers of this book will experience as they acquire coins for their collection.

Historical essays. Each of the women in this book has her own individual story, just as each of us does. I have long maintained that if we listen to someone for as few as 15 minutes, we will discover something about them that is unique, unusual, and even extraordinary. Unfortunately, we seldom take the time to listen. In this book, I tried to "listen" long enough to provide not just the mundane historical facts of these women's lives, but to reveal what made them special, unique, or outstanding. In almost every case, this was an easy task, and I learned that much of what I knew about some of these women was incorrect or incomplete, and that there were many things about them that I never knew. For instance, I had never heard that Prince Rainier asked for a $2 million dowry from Grace Kelly, that there were multiple Cleopatras, that Princess Diana had an eating disorder, or that Queen Hatshepsut of Egypt wore a false, pharaoh's beard. These were the sorts of discoveries that made writing this book such a pleasant experience.

Because of space considerations, narratives were limited to a certain number of words (425 for the first 10 women and 375 for the remaining 90). For the average woman, this presented no problem. In an ideal situation, the length of the historical narrative equaled that of the numismatic descriptions. However, such was almost never the case. Two extreme scenarios occurred 1) when there was scant biographical information about a woman and she appeared on few coins, and 2) when a woman left behind a rich historical record and she appeared on many coins. In the former situation, it was difficult to flesh out the narrative; in the latter, I needed more room. Thus, as you read this book you will notice that sometimes the historical narrative exceeds the size of the numismatic narrative and vice-versa. However, interesting stories and coins always took precedence.

Interesting Facts. In researching the women in this book, I came across interesting and unusual information that merited special mention. It might have been something about the life of the woman in question, or anything else related to her country, her relatives, or her legacy. For instance, I learned that Helen Keller was always photographed in profile because she had a bulging left eye, and that Lou Hoover never smiled in her photographs because she had a large gap between her front teeth, and that Susan B. Anthony's middle name was Brownell.

Collecting Difficulty. This section gives the reader a sense of how easy or difficult it is to obtain a coin of a particular woman. The scale is simple and consists of three levels: Easy, Moderately Difficult, and Difficult. The difficulty level is determined by two factors: how often a coin appears for sale, and its cost. It has little to do with mintages because, as I discovered, there are many coins with large mintages that rarely appear on the market, and there are many coins with small mintages that, for whatever reason, appear frequently. The difficulty levels are somewhat independent of value because value is not a determining factor in how often a coin appears for sale. There are many expensive coins that show up often (I call these "money" coins, because if you have enough money you can always find one). Most of the difficulty ratings are based on personal experience—if I had a hard time finding an example for this book, I suspect you'll have a hard time finding one for your collection. For instance, I had a very difficult time finding a coin with an image of Ingrid Bergman. The Gibraltar crown with her image is supposedly a common coin, but good luck trying to find one.

Occasionally, the difficulty level may be dual, such as "Easy to moderately difficult." This situation occurs when there is a wide discrepancy in pricing. While the easy option might represent the path of least resistance, the tougher option might lead to a more gratifying collecting experience. For example, the silver Nicaraguan 100-cordobas coin featuring Betsy Ross is easy to obtain. The exact same design appears on the gold Nicaraguan 2,000-cordobas coin, which is moderately difficult to obtain. Here, the presence of Betsy Ross on the coin becomes irrelevant and the focus goes more to the rarity, appearance, and value of the coin itself.

Collecting Women on Coins

Historically women have shunned numismatics as both collectors and dealers. Numismatics is a male-dominated arena, but there are no barriers to entry except desire and disposable income. So, why has numismatics failed to attract women? One reason is that women have had nothing to collect that they can call their own. Now, they do.

One of the purposes of this book is to spark an interest in collecting coins that depict women. Anyone desiring to collect women on coins should remember that your collection is your personal preference. You decide which coins you want to add to your collection and how much you are willing to spend to accomplish your goals. The only "right" way to collect is the way which pleases you.

Nevertheless, here are a few suggestions on ways to collect women on coins:

Collect one woman. Choose a woman who interests you and try to collect as many different coins or design types as possible. There are several women in this book who have appeared on numerous coins from a variety of countries, and who would form the basis for a rather extensive collection. For example, Queen Elizabeth II would make a phenomenal one-woman collection. Her appearances are so many, and so varied, that it would take years to acquire all the coins issued in her honor, and I doubt if such a collection could ever be completed. One of the benefits of a Queen Elizabeth collection is that many of the other women in this book appear on the opposite side of some of her coins. Also, keep in mind that many associated items can be added to flesh out a collection: medals, banknotes, tokens, images on postcards or stamps, etc.

Collect a theme. Do you like musicians? Athletes? Religious figures? These are just some of the types of themes that could form the basis for a specialized collection. The benefit of a thematic collection is that it will include coins from multiple countries. For example, a collection of dancers on coins could include a ribbon dancer from Austria and the Congo; ethnic Apsara, Katkah, and Legong dancers from Camdodia; folk dancers from Ukraine; ballerinas from Russia, Belarus, and France; and many others.

Collect a category. Pick one of the four categories identified in the survey: Allegorical Women, Real Women, Goddesses, or Women in Artwork. Meaningful collections can be built in any one of these categories. The smallest category, Women in Artwork, is visually impressive because the coins present some of the greatest art in history. The largest category, Real Women, is the most diverse and challenging. Each coin presents an actual woman who made a big impact on the historical record.

Collect all of the 100 Greatest Women on Coins. Why not attempt to obtain at least one coin of each of the 100 women who appear in this book? Having already engaged in this process in a quest for images, I can attest to the challenge, expense, and excitement involved in forming such a collection. For some women, the collector has multiple choices between coins that are expensive and inexpensive, rare and common, Uncirculated or Proof, base metal or precious metal, ancient or modern, and so many other competing variables. The majority of the coins in this set will be affordable, but a few are very rare and quite expensive. The end result would be a collection filled with fascinating stories and beautiful designs that even non-collectors could appreciate. As of this writing, the Professional Coin Grading Service (PCGS) is working on creating a Registry Set of the 100 Greatest Women so that collectors can list their collections and compete for completeness and quality.

Collect every woman who appears on a coin. Using the checklist in the back of this book, try to obtain one coin to represent every woman listed. I hesitate to suggest such a collection because it would be so vast and so challenging, but if you are looking for a lifetime of fun, this is the set for you. One of the side benefits of such a collection is the educational value. The natural response to obtaining a coin is to learn as much as possible about the woman who appears on it. As a result, you will learn about history, geography, economics, politics, and many associated topics.

How to Obtain Women on Coins

Currently, there is no central source for coins with women's portraits. Until demand for women on coins creates such a supplier, collectors must rely on a variety of means to obtain coins for their collections. Traditional sources of coins include brick-and-mortar coin shops and online venues, eBay, mail order, want lists, numismatic publications, international mints, modern-coin suppliers, and numismatic auctions. Many of the images in this book were taken of coins I obtained online, so I know from experience what you will be facing as you attempt to hunt down such coins. The best, easiest, and most useful site I found was eBay. Sometimes, a creative search was required, but I was able to locate and buy coins from all over the world on eBay, often choosing from a selection of various grades and prices.

Another good source is coin shows, which I like to view as an opportunity to visit multiple coin "shops" in one day. Local shows are smaller gatherings, with fewer opportunities to purchase coins with women's portraits, but they are convenient because they are close and it is an excellent way to make contacts with dealers who might be able to help you fill your want list in the future. Regional shows are much larger and will have a more diverse selection of dealers, giving you more opportunities to obtain coins for your collection. However, regional shows require more expense and time just to travel there and see everyone. National shows are among the largest in the world and the selections there are usually sufficient to exhaust your collecting budget. National shows include the American Numismatic Association's annual summer convention (held in rotating cities in August of each year), the Florida United Numismatists annual convention (held in Orlando or Tampa each January), the Whitman Coin & Collectibles Expo (held in Baltimore, Maryland, three times a year in March, July, and November), and the Long Beach Expo (held in Long Beach, California, three times a year in February, June, and September). Once again, travel expenses and time commitments increase for national shows. International coin shows offer the widest selection of coins with women's portraits simply because they are a gathering of dealers who specialize in world coins, both ancient and modern, and who are most likely to offer many of the coins in this book.

In the United States, the only two international coins shows are the New York International Numismatic Convention (held in New York every January) and the Chicago International Coin Fair (held in Chicago each April). For a complete listing of upcoming coin shows, visit the Numismaster Web site at www.numismaster.com/ta/inside_numis.jsp?page=CoinShowsCalendar.

A Word About Pricing

The value or worth of a coin is strictly a function of supply and demand. Whatever the prices are today for women on coins, they will rise in the future as this book creates a new level of demand for such coins. Your style of collecting will determine how much you are willing to pay for a given coin. If you are patient, you can find good values. If you are in a rush, you will pay a premium for your impatience. When purchasing coins for this book, I experienced the same phenomenon—I always paid more for the coins I needed quickly because I did not have the time to shop as carefully as I normally would. Also, if I had a choice between a U.S. seller and an overseas seller, I would often choose the U.S. seller even if the coin cost more, not because I was "buying American" but because I knew the coin would arrive sooner.

While catalogs such as the Krause-Mishler *Standard Catalog of World Coins* do an excellent job of valuing hundreds of thousands of coins, there is often a big disparity between the catalog value and the actual price you may have to pay. This is especially true in the market for modern coins, where a high percentage of the 100 Greatest Women on Coins originated.

Final Thoughts

Please send any comments, corrections, suggestions, and (especially) new women on coins to:

Ron Guth
4640 Cass Street #9119
San Diego CA 92169-7006
Phone: 858-349-8270
Email: ron@germancoins.com

100 GREATEST WOMEN ON COINS

No. 1

MARY, MOTHER OF JESUS

Mary's story is told in the Christian Bible, where she is portrayed as the mother of Jesus the Messiah. According to the biblical account in the books of Matthew and Luke, Mary and her cousin Elizabeth experienced miraculous conceptions. Elizabeth, barren and old, became pregnant and gave birth to John "The Baptist." Six months after Elizabeth became pregnant, an angel visited Mary, a young virgin engaged to Joseph, to announce that she would be impregnated by the Holy Spirit. Her fiancé, understandably upset, sought to break off the engagement, but was likewise convinced by an angel of the special nature of the child she carried. Mary gave birth to Jesus while on a trip to Bethlehem to register for a census. The local inns were full of people on similar missions, forcing Mary to give birth to Jesus in a barn. Later, Mary witnessed Jesus's first miracle when he turned water into wine at a wedding party in Cana. She was present at his crucifixion and death, and she was with his apostles when they met together after his death.

In the Christian faith, Mary is revered as the mother of the Christ-child. In the Catholic faith, Mary holds a special place of honor as a saint. The Hail Mary, oft-repeated by Roman Catholics, reinforces her standing in that religion. In the Muslim Quran, Mary (Maryam) occupies the 19th chapter, where the virgin birth is described.

Mary is one of the few women who have appeared in more than one category (see the introduction) and, with a bit of a stretch, she can be nudged into all four categories. She has appeared on coins as a *Real Woman* (although all portraits of her are imagined, as no contemporary portrait of her exists). Most often, she appears with her newborn child. She is included in the *Women in Art* category, thanks to the countless depictions of her in religious art such as Renaissance paintings, sculpture, and Russian icons. Some feminists include Mary as a *Goddess*, citing Mariolatry or Marian devotion both within and outside of the Church. In the sense that Mary represents the abstract notions of purity, chastity, motherhood, and devotion, she is also an *Allegorical Woman*.

In numismatics, Mary has appeared on countless coins over the centuries. Some of the more interesting examples include the Liberian 2007 $5 coin that features the Black Madonna of Częstochowa, complete with the scars on her face inflicted by Hussite robbers in 1430 AD. The 1936 Austrian 5-schilling coin features a stylized version of Mary and Jesus, both in a triangular shape. The Fiji 2013 $2 coin depicts the "Theotokos of the Seven Arrows" icon, in which Mary is pierced by seven arrows, representing the seven sorrows of her life.

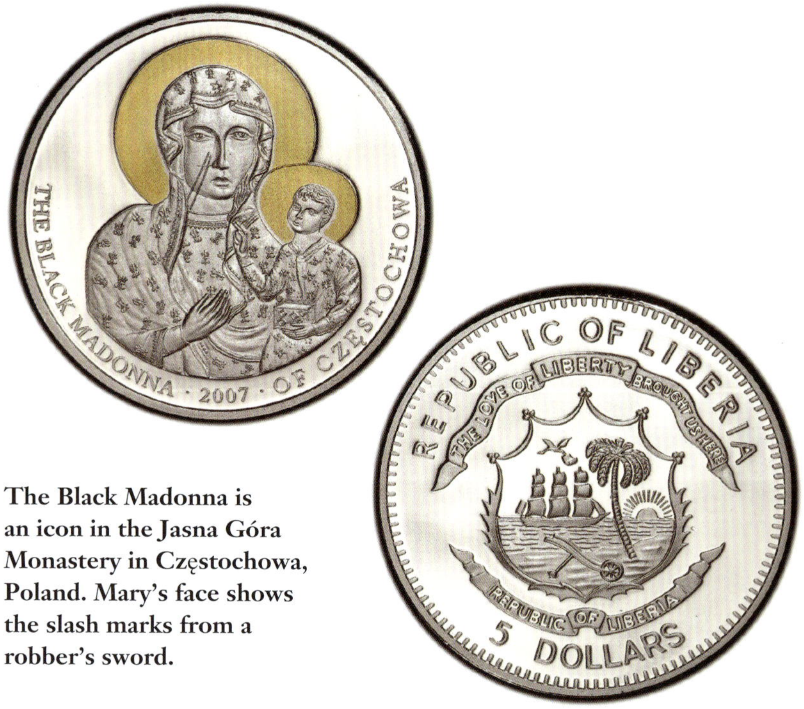

The Black Madonna is an icon in the Jasna Góra Monastery in Częstochowa, Poland. Mary's face shows the slash marks from a robber's sword.

COLLECTING DIFFICULTY

Easy. Collectors have hundreds of different opportunities to acquire a coin with a portrait of Mary, including a lengthy series of "Madonna" thalers issued by the German region of Bavaria from the 1600s through the 1700s. This series includes some of the most affordable thalers of their respective eras. A collection composed just of the different Marian coin types would be simultaneously daunting, challenging, and rewarding.

1

The Virgin in Prayer, by Giovanni Battista da Sassoferrato, circa 1640–1650.

Nicephorus II Phocas (963–969 AD). The Virgin Mary is seen on the reverse, wearing a nimbus crown and holding a stola and maphorium.

Constantine X Ducas (1059–1067 AD). Here Mary is portrayed on the obverse, accompanied by the emperor Constantine on the reverse.

No. 2

HELEN KELLER

Helen Keller was a remarkable woman who overcame her blindness and deafness to become one of the most inspirational figures in American history. Most people know her from the 1962 movie *The Miracle Worker*, which portrayed the relationship between Helen (played by Patty Duke) and her teacher, Anne Sullivan (played by Anne Bancroft). In one dramatic scene, Helen finally makes the connection between the word "water" and the liquid flowing over her hands, thus opening up for her a whole new world. In her book, *The Story of My Life*, Helen described that moment: "That living word awakened my soul, gave it light, hope, joy, set it free."

Helen was born in July 1880 in Tuscumbia, Alabama, and started out life as any normal child. Before her second birthday, she became ill with an unexplained fever (some say scarlet) which left her blind and deaf. Thereafter she communicated with her family using rudimentary signing, but she became increasingly frustrated and willful. On a trip to visit an eye specialist, the doctor recommended the family contact Alexander Graham Bell, the inventor of the telephone, who in turn led them to the Perkins School for the Blind in Boston and, eventually, to Anne Sullivan.

Early images of Helen Keller invariably show her in profile to hide her bulging left eye. When she was 30, doctors removed both her eyes and replaced them with glass prosthetics.

Under Anne's tutelage and companionship, Helen grew up into an accomplished woman. She attended Radcliffe College and became, in 1904, the first deaf-blind person ever to earn a Bachelor of Arts degree. She wrote numerous inspirational essays and books, and she lectured around the world on women's suffrage, socialism, and peace. In 1915 she co-founded Helen Keller International, which still exists today and serves to prevent blindness, malnutrition, and disability.

Helen Keller was an avowed socialist and championed the working class. She was a member of the "Wobblies" (International Workers of the World) and campaigned actively for workers' rights. One of the motivating factors of her activism was her discovery that blindness was, in many cases, preventable.

Surprisingly few numismatic items depict Helen Keller. The reverse of the 2003 United States Mint 50 State Quarters® Program coin for Alabama shows her seated in a chair reading a book in Braille. Her name appears in the field to the right in both English and Braille—this was the first time the tactile writing system appeared on a U.S. coin. Helen also appears on several medallic issues, in much higher relief than on the quarter.

Alabama honored Helen Keller on a special State quarter. This was the first use of Braille on a U.S. coin.

COLLECTING DIFFICULTY

Easy. The 2003 "Keller" quarter is available in large quantities in both Mint State and Proof at affordable prices (and circulated examples can be collected at face value from pocket change). Proof versions in silver command a slight premium; they can be purchased for less than $10.

Helen Keller, circa 1904.

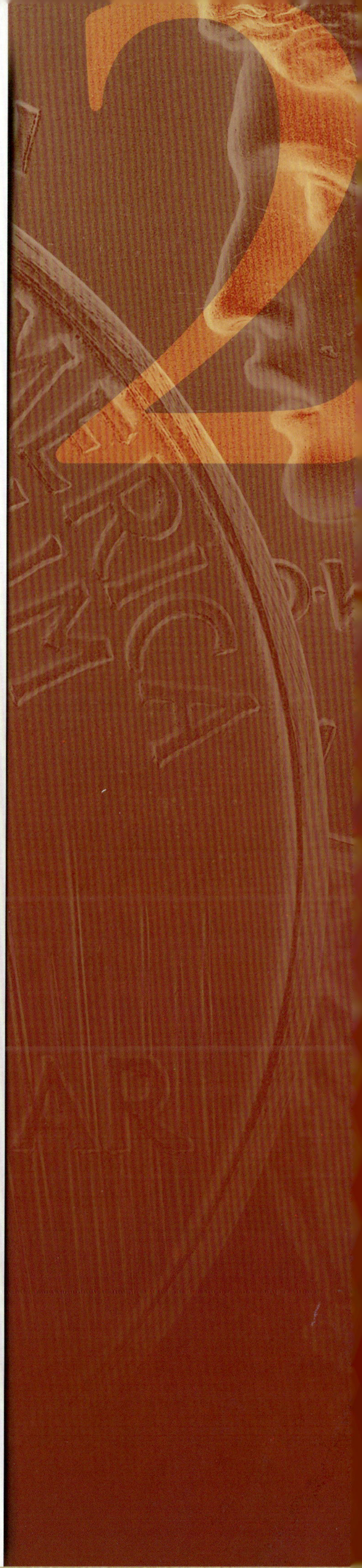

No. 3

MOTHER TERESA

Mother Teresa is best known for her selfless devotion to the poor, the outcast, the sick, and the dying, primarily in her adopted country of India.

Anjezë (Agnes) Gonxhe Bojaxhiu was born in 1910 in the small town of Skopje in what is now the country of Macedonia. She developed a desire to enter religious life at an early age and became a novitiate with the Sisters of Loreto at the age of 18. She learned English in Ireland and then went to Darjeeling, India, to begin her service as a missionary. The young nun took her religious vows on May 24, 1931, choosing the name Teresa after Saint Thérèse of Lisieux, the patron saint of missionaries.

In Calcutta, India, Mother Teresa changed her focus from teaching to serving poor slum-dwellers. In 1950 she began the Missionaries of Charity, which has since grown to include more than 4,500 members in over 100 countries. In recognition of her efforts, she received the Nobel Peace Prize in 1979. She unselfishly donated the prize money—about $190,000 U.S.—to the poor.

Many books have been written by and about Mother Teresa. One of her own books, *In the Heart of the World*, contains 28 thoughts, stories, and prayers that provide a window into her life of faith and service. She wrote of love and humility, but, more importantly, she practiced what she preached and served as a living example to others.

Mother Teresa stood only five feet tall. Instead of wearing the traditional habit of their order, she and the Missionaries of Charity wore white saris of widowhood with a border of three blue lines.

In her extensive travels throughout the world, Mother Teresa encountered and became friends with several of the other 100 Greatest Women. In 1976 Indira Gandhi (no. 75) conferred on her a Doctorate of Literature. In 1983 Queen Elizabeth II (no. 12) presented her with Britain's Honorary Order of Merit. Princess Diana (no. 6) met with Mother Teresa on more than one occasion; the two women would die six days apart.

On September 5, 1997, Mother Teresa passed away after several years of heart problems. The Republic of India afforded her a full state funeral. Tens of thousands of people watched as her body was transported through the streets on the same carriage used for Mahatma Gandhi's funeral in 1948.

Mother Teresa appears on coins from several countries, including India, France, and the British Virgin Islands. In 2010 India issued a 5-rupee coin to commemorate the 100th anniversary of her birth—supposedly, five rupees was all the money she carried in her pocket when she left for medical training in Patna, India, as part of her preparation of ministry to the poor.

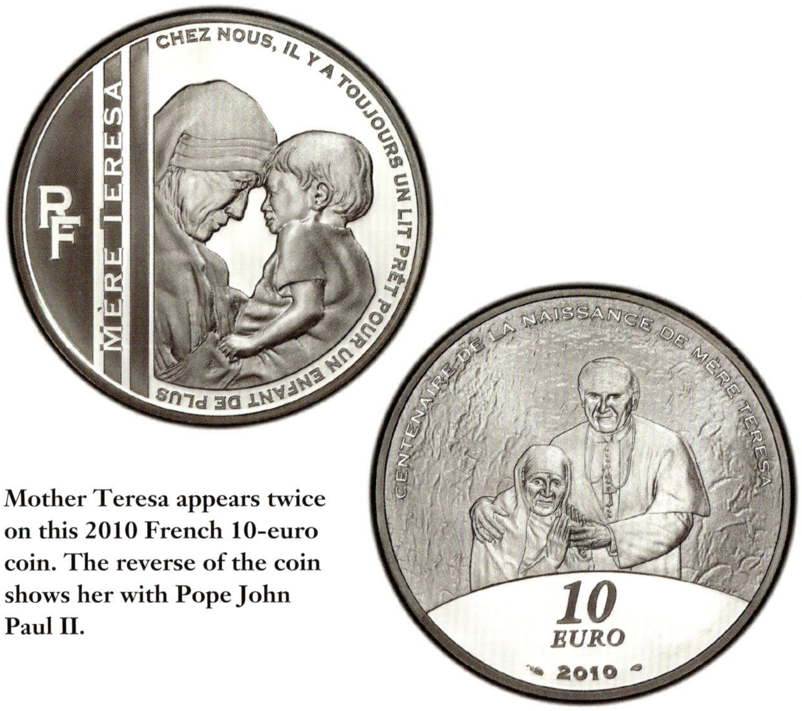

Mother Teresa appears twice on this 2010 French 10-euro coin. The reverse of the coin shows her with Pope John Paul II.

COLLECTING DIFFICULTY

Easy. Prices range from just a few dollars for the India 5-rupee coin to around $100 for special silver commemorative coins.

A United States postage stamp printed in 2010.

Mother Teresa appears on the obverse of this 2010 Mumbai 5-rupee coin celebrating the 100th anniversary of her birth.

No. 4

QUEEN CLEOPATRA (OR CLEOPATRA VII PHILOPATOR)

Cleopatra was said to be one of the most beautiful women of the ancient world. She was a queen of Egypt who turned the heads of Roman emperors, one of whom gave up his empire for her. Many people know Cleopatra only as Elizabeth Taylor, the actress who played the devastatingly beautiful queen in the 1963 eponymous movie.

Cleopatra at most was only half-Egyptian and may have been entirely Greek. She descended from a line of rulers that began with Ptolemy I, who hailed from Macedonia, a region in northern Greece. Cleopatra's father, Ptolemy XII, stood eighth in line in the family dynasty. Nor was Cleopatra the only child of her lineage so-named. Her mother was most likely Cleopatra V Tryphaena, and her daughter was Cleopatra Selene II. As if the whole Ptolemy/Cleopatra naming conventions weren't confusing enough, Cleopatra VII ruled at various times with four Ptolemies: her father, Ptolemy XII; her brothers, Ptolemy XIII and XIV, both of whom she married; and her son, Ptolemy XV Caesarion.

Cleopatra had a particular fondness for poisons. She allegedly poisoned her brother and husband, Ptolemy XIV, to assume sole power in Egypt. She tested various poisons on live subjects and, by most accounts, committed suicide by allowing an Egyptian cobra to bite her.

By most accounts, Cleopatra held sway over her suitors with her beauty, her voice, and her mannerisms. She married three times, twice to her younger brothers (both times for political reasons) and once to Mark Antony. Her first big romance was with Julius Caesar, who conquered the Egyptian capitol, Alexandria, in 48 BC. and was himself captivated by Cleopatra. Together they had a son, Ptolemy XV Caesarion ("Little Caesar") in 47 BC. Cleopatra was in Rome with her son when assassins killed Julius Caesar. She returned to Alexandria and then began a relationship with Mark Antony, by whom she had twins, Alexander Helios and Cleopatra Selene II. A few years later, Cleopatra and Mark Antony married and had another son, Ptolemy XVI Philadelphus.

Cleopatra can be seen on numerous coins of both ancient and modern Egypt. Her portrait on the reverse of a silver denarius (with an obverse of Mark Antony) represents the first time a foreign head of state appeared on a Roman coin. She appears by herself on a bronze 40-drachma coin issued between 51 and 30 BC. In 1993 Egypt issued a gold 50-pound coin featuring Cleopatra on the obverse, where she is shown wearing a royal vulture headdress.

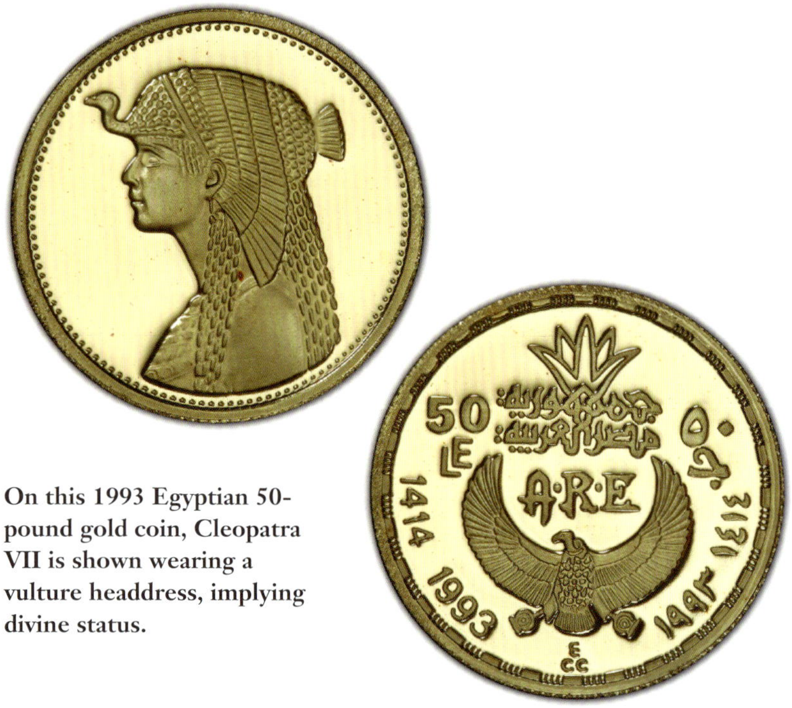

On this 1993 Egyptian 50-pound gold coin, Cleopatra VII is shown wearing a vulture headdress, implying divine status.

COLLECTING DIFFICULTY

Easy. Surprisingly, the selection of ancient Cleopatra coins is greater than that of the moderns. Low-grade examples of ancient Cleopatra coins are notably inexpensive ($200 to $800) and can be found with ease either online, in auctions, or in the inventories of dealers who specialize in ancient coins. Beware of counterfeits, and deal only with reputable sources.

4

Cleopatra VII statue fragment, 69–30 BC.

From the Ptolemaic Kingdom, featuring Cleopatra VII, 51–30 BC.

A silver denarius featuring both Cleopatra VII and Marc Antony, 32 BC.

No. 5

SUSAN B. ANTHONY

Susan B. Anthony was one of the most influential female figures in American politics in the 19th century. She is known primarily as a suffragist, but she was also an active participant in the temperance and abolitionist movements.

Susan (as she was referred to by her good friend, Elizabeth Cady Stanton) was born in 1820 in Adams, Massachusetts. Her first job was as a teacher, where she noted the sometimes large disparity in pay between men and women. Early in her reform efforts, Susan worked for the anti-slavery movement, then focused on the temperance movement. Her real passion became the women's movement: not just for voting rights but also for legal rights. One of the hindrances to the women's reform movement was a lack of money, primarily because women had no money of their own and little control over their family finances. Susan fought for a woman's rights to divorce, to inherit, and to keep property.

During the Civil War, as the country's attention turned to the anti-slavery movement, the women's movement was asked to take a back seat and wait its turn. Susan resisted. In fact, she opposed the Fifteenth Amendment because it granted voting rights to black men but omitted women.

The "B" in Susan's name stands for Brownell. The 19th Amendment to the U.S. Constitution is sometimes referred to as the Anthony Amendment.

In 1872 Susan was arrested and tried for voting. A judge (male, of course, as was the norm at the time) found her guilty and fined her $100, but Susan vowed never to pay the fine—a promise she kept. In 1878 the first attempt to pass a constitutional amendment guaranteeing women the right to vote failed in the Senate; it was not until 1920 that the amendment became law. Susan B. Anthony, who died in 1906, never saw the fruition of her life's work.

In various times in her life, Susan came into contact with other famous figures from the reform movements, including Lucretia Mott, the Grimke sisters, Harriet Tubman, Sojourner Truth, Lucy Stone, and Frederick Douglass. She met Elizabeth Cady Stanton in 1851, and they became lifelong friends and inseparable collaborators.

In 1979 the United States honored Susan with a special $1 coin. The portrait on the coin captured her distinctive angular nose, jutting chin, and bun hairdo. Though minted in large quantities from 1979 to 1981, and again in a final mintage of more than 40 million coins in 1999, the "SBA" dollar never caught on with the general public, partly because of its confusing size (it was larger than a quarter but smaller than a half dollar).

In 1979 Susan B. Anthony, the great American suffragist, appeared on a new U.S. $1 coin. Though unpopular because of its odd size, the coin introduced Susan to millions of new fans.

COLLECTING DIFFICULTY

Easy. Susan B. Anthony dollars are among the most common U.S. coins and are available for just a small premium over their face value.

Susan B. Anthony, 1890s.

No. 6

PRINCESS DIANA

Princess Diana was one of the most visible, beloved, and tragic members of the British royal family. She was born The Honourable Diana Frances Spencer in July 1961. She led a fairly normal, albeit aristocratic, youth. When her father inherited the title of Earl in 1975, she became known as Lady Diana Frances Spencer. Diana met her future husband, Charles, Prince of Wales, when he dated her older sister, Lady Sarah Spencer. The prince's attention turned to Diana in 1980, and, after a quick courtship, the couple announced their engagement in February 1981.

The fairy-tale wedding of Princess Diana and Prince Charles took place at Westminster Abbey on July 29, 1981, shortly after Diana's 20th birthday. The event was attended by 3,500 guests and was watched by 750 million viewers around the world. Upon their marriage, Diana's title became Her Royal Highness, the Princess of Wales.

Diana and Charles had two sons, Prince William and Prince Harry. The relationship between the couple disintegrated over time, culminating in a divorce in August 1996, 15 years after their marriage. In a 1995 interview with Martin Bashir for *Panorama* on the BBC, Diana blamed the failure of her marriage on the pressures of her position within the royal family, media attention, and her husband's rekindled relationship with his ex-girlfriend, Camilla Parker-Bowles (whom he later married).

The train on Diana's wedding dress was 25 feet long. Diana suffered from self-avowed bulimia, and she alluded to cutting (deliberate self-harm), both brought on by low self-esteem and the trouble in her marriage.

Diana met or knew several other women who have appeared on coins, including Mother Teresa (no. 3 among the 100 Greatest), Queen Elizabeth II (no. 12), and Sarah Ferguson (not ranked in the 100 Greatest).

In August 1997, Diana died as a result of a car accident in which she, her boyfriend Dodi Fayed, and the driver were killed.

Princess Diana is one of the most popular subjects on modern coins, and she appears on numerous issues from scores of countries. Two events spurred a flurry of new Diana coins: her marriage to Charles in 1981, and her death in 1997. For her marriage in 1981, Great Britain issued a large 25-pence coin in both copper-nickel and silver. It featured Diana and Charles on the reverse. For her death, Great Britain struck 5-pound coins in copper-nickel, silver, and gold in 1999, "In Memory of Diana." Ironically, given their often strained personal relationship, Queen Elizabeth appears on the opposite side of the coin. Most of the countries that issued marriage coins also produced coins to record the princess's death, and it appears that there are more death coins than marriage coins because of the incredible popularity she attracted.

Two years after her death, Great Britain issued a gold 5-pound coin honoring Princess Diana. Notice whose head is larger.

COLLECTING DIFFICULTY

Easy, because of the large variety of coins that bear her image. Prices range from less than $5 for the most common coins to thousands of dollars for the gold versions. A collection of Princess Diana coins would be both extensive and not that expensive.

A United Kingdom postage stamp printed in 1998.

Pure-gold memorial coin from the United Kingdom.

Australian 50-cent coin with images of Diana and Prince Charles on the reverse.

No. 7

BETSY ROSS

Tradition ascribes the first American flag to a young seamstress named Betsy Ross. For centuries, schoolchildren have been taught that Betsy, in collaboration with some of the Founding Fathers, designed and created the first flag. However, skeptics and historians question the truth of this time-honored story.

Betsy Ross was born Elizabeth Pheobe Griscom in January 1752 in Philadelphia, Pennsylvania. "Betsy" became her nickname as a child, and the Ross surname was that of her first husband. She grew up in a Quaker household, where she learned sewing from her great-aunt. Later she apprenticed with an upholsterer, William Webster, in his shop, which is where she met her husband, John Ross. At 21, Betsy and John eloped and started their own upholstery business. Shortly thereafter, the American Revolutionary War broke out, and John died in a munitions accident. Betsy married twice more. She survived all of her husbands.

Betsy Ross was born on March 1, 1752, but the change from the Julian calendar to the Gregorian calendar in that year changed her birth date to January 1. Her mother, her father, and a sister died in 1793 in the yellow-fever epidemic, the same one that closed the Philadelphia Mint in its first year of operation. Betsy's daughter, Mary, made the Star-Spangled Banner, the flag that flew over Fort McHenry in 1814 and which inspired America's national anthem.

The Betsy Ross flag legend recounts that George Washington, Robert Morris, and George Ross (no relation), all three representing the Continental Congress, visited Betsy in 1776 to discuss creating a national flag. During their consultation, she suggested a five-pointed star instead of a six-pointed one, and she demonstrated to the men how to quickly fold and cut one from a piece of cloth. Betsy's final flag—the one that became the emblem of the new nation—showed a circle of 13 five-pointed stars on a blue background and 13 horizontal stripes of red and white.

Unfortunately, no documentation exists to prove this story. Skeptics claim the timing of the events is implausible or that Francis Hopkinson was the true creator of the first flag. Others note that the legend did not arise until 1870, when Betsy's grandson, William J. Canby, made the claim that she created the first flag. In spite of this doubt, the legend continues, with adherents on both sides.

The Ross flag legend has been depicted on stamps, in artwork, in books, and on coins. Surprisingly, no coin of the United States recognizes Betsy Ross and this momentous event. Collectors must go to Nicaraguan coins or medallic issues to obtain an image of this American icon.

Betsy Ross has never appeared on a U.S. coin, but Nicaragua paid her homage on the 1975 100-cordoba piece. She appears opposite an astronaut planting an American flag on the moon.

COLLECTING DIFFICULTY

Easy, but the choices are limited. The Nicaraguan 100-cordoba coins of 1975 are the least expensive option; these portray Betsy stitching a flag in conjunction with an astronaut planting an American flag on the moon. Uncirculated examples run around $40 to $50, and Proof examples sell for slightly more.

Betsy Ross showing Major Ross and Robert Morris how she cut the stars for the American flag; George Washington sits in a chair on the left. This painting is by Jean Leon Gerome Ferris.

This silvered-brass medal represents the 1926 U.S. sesquicentennial and features the Betsy Ross House, Philadelphia, on the obverse.

No. 8

MARTHA WASHINGTON

Martha Washington, the first First Lady of the United States, was born Martha Dandridge in June 1731 in what was then the British province of Virginia. She married her first husband, Daniel Parker Custis, in 1750. She was 18 and he was 38. Martha bore four children before Daniel died in 1757. Upon his death, when Martha was 25, she became a rich widow with numerous plantations and hundreds of slaves. Many of these she brought with her in 1759 to her marriage to a young Army colonel, George Washington, himself a wealthy landowner. Together they settled at Washington's Mount Vernon home on the Potomac River south of Alexandria, Virginia. Their house and farm survive to this day as a national historic landmark and a popular tourist destination.

During the Revolutionary War, Martha spent several years with George at the army's winter encampments at Valley Forge, sometimes enduring days of travel over hundreds of miles to join her husband. Once there, she hosted dinner engagements, attended camp plays, and socialized with the officers and their ladies. The soldiers bestowed upon her the unofficial title "Lady Washington."

The female portrait on the obverses of the 1792 half dismes and 1792 Birch cents (which were U.S. prototype coins) appears similar to that of Martha Washington, and some researchers asserted that connection in the past. However, modern research debunks that theory in favor of them being a generic symbolic portrait of Miss Liberty.

Martha opposed George's acceptance of the presidency of the new United States, preferring instead that he remain at Mount Vernon. Supposedly, she refused to attend his first inauguration. Eventually, despite feeling lonely and out of place in the first national capitals of New York and Philadelphia, Martha begrudgingly accepted her role as First Lady and remained faithful to her duties and to her husband. After the presidency the couple returned to Mount Vernon, where, instead of relaxing in their final years, they hosted a seemingly endless stream of visitors, much to Martha's irritation.

Martha Washington appears on only one non-pattern American coin—the 2007-W $10 "First Spouse" coin. The obverse features a bust of Martha in a hair bonnet; the reverse shows her seated, engaged in mending what appears to be her husband's uniform coat. The legend around the reverse reads "First Lady of the Continental Army," a title given by soldiers in recognition of her frequent visits. Martha appears on some experimental pattern coins (back-dated 1759 but actually produced in the 1960s and beyond), but these are rarely seen and are quite valuable. She also appears on the United States $1 Silver Certificate bank note and on two U.S. postage stamps. Invariably, Martha is portrayed as a matronly, stout, perhaps frumpy woman, but modern feminist historians have begun to reinterpret her as young, intelligent, and strong-minded.

Martha Washington died in 1802, outliving her husband by two years.

The first U.S. First Lady appears on the first First Spouse coin. The reverse is an imagined portrayal of Martha on one of her visits to George Washington's army encampments.

COLLECTING DIFFICULTY

Easy, but slightly expensive. The Martha Washington "First Spouse" coin contains half an ounce of pure gold. An inexpensive alternative is a 1976 Mardi Gras token that shows a young Martha on the obverse paired rather incongruously with a Venus de Milo on the reverse (these can be found online for less than $10).

Martha Dandridge Custis Washington, by Eliphalet Frazer Andrews, circa 1878.

The 1759-dated "Martha Washington" die has been used to test coinage alloys at the Mint since 1965. The design omits the denomination and the legend UNITED STATES OF AMERICA.

No. 9

JACQUELINE "JACKIE" KENNEDY

Known for her elegance and poise, Jacqueline Kennedy became one of the most popular First Ladies in American history. She was a fashion icon who brought a whole new level of young sophistication to the role of First Lady. Through her efforts and fundraising, the White House underwent a major redecoration that turned it from a home for the president and his family to an historic house for the American people.

"Jackie" Kennedy was born Jacqueline Lee Bouvier in July 1929. As a young child she became an accomplished equestrienne and enjoyed life in high society. She attended Vassar College, the University of Grenoble, the Sorbonne, and George Washington University, ultimately earning an undergraduate degree in French literature.

In her 2014 biography of Jacqueline Kennedy, author Barbara Leaming makes the case that Jackie suffered from post-traumatic stress disorder (PTSD) resulting from the assassination of her husband.

In September 1953, Jackie married U.S. senator John F. Kennedy, who became president in 1960. America was fascinated by this attractive young couple. Jackie became an important public-relations asset to JFK. Her knowledge of French history and her ability to speak the language boosted America's prestige when the pair visited France in 1961. After her husband's assassination in 1963, Jackie created the Camelot myth that likened their time in the White House to the Arthurian legend.

Jackie's, as well as America's, life was shattered on November 23, 1963, when Lee Harvey Oswald shot and killed the president. Most people alive at the time remember exactly where they were when they heard the news that President Kennedy had been shot. They also remember the images of Jackie, stoic in her black mourning dress, as she and her children stood at her husband's grave.

In 1968 Jackie married Greek shipping magnate Aristotle Onassis and became known as "Jackie O." Following Aristotle's death in 1975, she became a book editor and spearheaded historic preservation efforts in Washington, D.C., and New York City. She died in May 1994 from non-Hodgkin's lymphoma.

As popular as Jackie was in real life, she appears on few coins. Liberia issued a $10 coin in 2002 featuring a bust of Jackie with a smaller bust of JFK beside her. Up to 2015, America had yet to issue a coin honoring the First Lady, but that oversight was corrected in 2015 with the issuance of her First Spouse gold bullion coin. In recognition of Jackie's popularity, the Mint tripled the mintage of her coin relative to the other three issues of the year. Jackie is also seen on the bronze First Spouse medal issued in conjunction with her First Spouse coin.

Jackie Kennedy's First Spouse coin features the saucer magnolia which she selected for the White House and her husband's grave.

COLLECTING DIFFICULTY

Moderate. Coins depicting Jackie Kennedy are not particularly rare—they are just difficult to find. Considering how popular Jackie was, it is surprising that she does not appear on more coins. Hopefully, the 2015 issuance of her First Spouse coin will attract new collectors, but with half an ounce of gold in each coin, they will be expensive.

Jacqueline throwing the bouquet at her wedding to John F. Kennedy.

9

No. 10

EMPRESS CATHERINE II (OR CATHERINE THE GREAT)

Catherine II, also known as Catherine the Great, became one of the most influential rulers of the Russian Empire. However, she wasn't a native-born Russian at all; she was the daughter of Christian August, Prince of the German state of Anhalt-Zerbst, and Johanna Elisabeth of Holstein-Gottorp, located in present-day Germany and Denmark. In fact, she was born Sophie Friederike Auguste von Anhalt-Zerbst-Dornburg in April 1729.

At age 15, Princess Sophie travelled to Russia, where she immediately ingratiated herself to the Empress Elizabeth. Sophie learned the Russian language and joined the Russian Orthodox Church, where she received her new name, Catherine (or Ekaterina in Russian). In 1745, at the age of 16, Catherine wed Peter von Holstein-Gottorp, Empress Elizabeth's nephew and her chosen successor. When Elizabeth died in 1762, Peter became emperor of Russia as Peter III. He soon fell out of favor with the Russians because of his favoritism toward the Germans and, just six months into his reign, he fell victim to his wife's bloodless coup d'etat. On September 22, 1762, Catherine crowned herself empress of Russia.

The Principal Diamond Expert and Court Jeweller, Jérémie Pauzié, created the Imperial Crown of Russia specifically for Catherine the Great's coronation. This remarkable crown boasts 75 pearls, nearly 5,000 diamonds, and a 398.62 carat ruby spinel. The same crown was worn by every subsequent Russian emperor until Nicholas II's forced abdication in 1917.

Catherine promoted the modernization of Russia in a period known as the Russian Enlightenment. This included aggressive foreign policy, political reforms, secularization of Church properties, importing Western culture, establishing the all-girl Smol'nyi Institute, increasing manufacturing and agriculture, and educational reforms. She expanded Russia's borders into Poland and took over the Crimean peninsula in 1783.

During her life, Catherine took numerous lovers, one of the foremost being Grigori Potemkin, with whom she may have had a clandestine marriage. Her sexual appetite gave rise to numerous scandalous rumors, including the questionable paternity of her son, Paul, and a false rumor about the circumstances of her death (the more mundane reality is that she died of a stroke).

Catherine's image appears on all the gold and silver Russian coins, including the large-sized roubles, from 1762 until her death in 1796. Collectors gravitate to Catherine's rouble coinage because she issued coins in every year of her reign. The design of her roubles, with minor modifications, remained the same throughout: a crowned bust of Catherine facing right on the obverse and a double-headed imperial eagle on the reverse. Copper coins issued during her reign bear her crowned monogram.

Mongolia and the Netherlands Antilles are two countries that have issued modern coins bearing Catherine the Great's likeness.

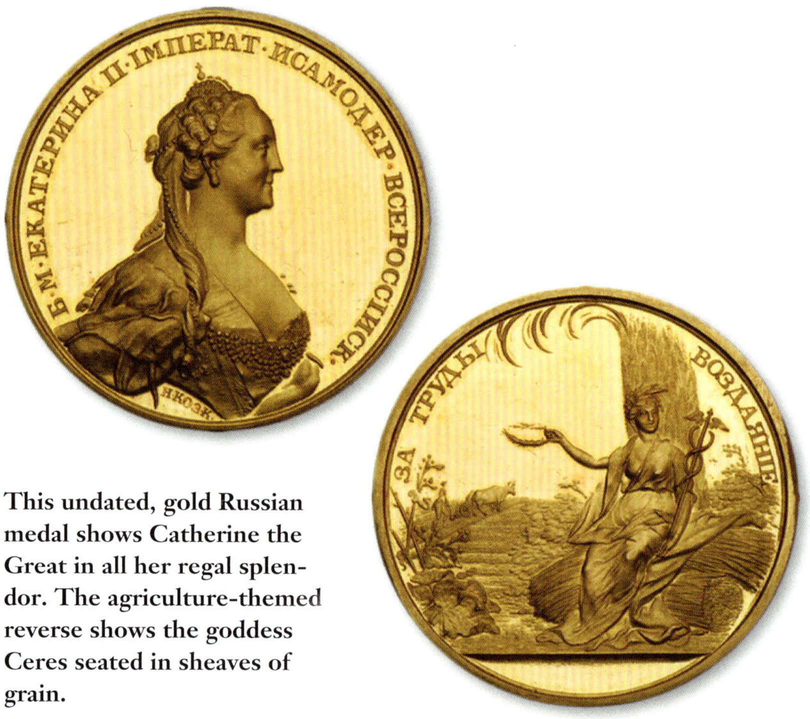

This undated, gold Russian medal shows Catherine the Great in all her regal splendor. The agriculture-themed reverse shows the goddess Ceres seated in sheaves of grain.

COLLECTING DIFFICULTY

Easy. Low-grade roubles from Catherine's reign are among the most affordable large-sized silver coins of their era. Decent examples can be found ranging in price from $250 to $750. Conversely, high-grade examples of all the Russian Catherine types become very expensive and are among the hottest commodities in the world-coin market today.

Empress Catherine the Great of Russia, by Fyodor Rokotov, circa 1763.

Catherine II appears on the obverse of this gold 10-rouble coin dated 1766. It is among the largest of all pre-1800 Russian gold coins.

A coin of unknown date features Catherine II facing right. This 20-kopeck coin came from the Moscow Mint.

No. 11

LIBERTY

In 1792 the American Congress legislated that all U.S. coins must bear a female representation of Liberty. This lasted until 1851, when a star and shield became the emblems on the three-cent silver pieces.

American Liberty reaching for her sword in a World War I poster.

Liberty, the female personification of freedom, dates back to ancient Greek and Roman times. The Greeks knew her as Eleutheria. The Romans called her Libertas.

An early appearance of the goddess Libertas was on a Roman denarius issued by the moneyer Q. Caepio Brutus in the year 54 BC. In this simple portrait, Libertas appears as a young woman, her hair up and jewelry dangling from her ear and around her neck. Her full name appears in the field behind her head.

During the American and French revolutions, Liberty became the favored alternative to the monarchial portraits on coins. In 1782 Benjamin Franklin proposed a medal to commemorate the American victories at the Battles of Saratoga and Yorktown. The obverse of the *Libertas Americana* medal featured a head of Liberty, her locks of hair flowing behind. The U.S. Liberty Cap half cents and cents of 1793 borrowed heavily from the design on this medal.

The evolution of Miss Liberty on American coins is fascinating to explore. In some portraits, she appears as a young woman with unkempt hair. In others she is quite fashionable, no doubt reflecting the styles of the time. In many designs, only her head is shown. Occasionally she shows some décolletage, and sometimes she is shown as a figure seated on a rock formation. In the most dramatic representations, Liberty is shown striding confidently across the coin or directly toward the viewer. Today, she remains a ubiquitous figure on the hundreds of millions of American silver and gold bullion coins that have been struck since 1986.

Miss Liberty as a design element is, by no means, solely an American concept. Countries such as Liberia, North Peru, pre-Communist Cuba, France, Haiti, and many others have often displayed their version of a female Liberty on coins. A rather large and varied collection could be built around the Miss Liberty theme.

Liberty is described as the "parent of science and industry" on the 1792 American pattern one-cent piece. In January 2015, the example pictured here sold at auction for $2,585,000.

COLLECTING DIFFICULTY

Easy. Whether from ancient or modern times, coins featuring Liberty are accessible and affordable.

Queen Elizabeth II has appeared on more coins than any other real woman in history. In terms of the total number of coins produced with her image, the number of countries that have produced coins bearing her portrait, or the sheer number of different types and designs, Queen Elizabeth wins in every category. Helen of Troy's face may have launched a thousand ships, but Queen Elizabeth's face has adorned billions of coins.

When the future Queen Elizabeth II was born in April 1926, the chances of her ascending to the throne of England were anything but assured. In line ahead of her were her uncle, the Prince of Wales (the future King Edward VIII), and her father, Prince Albert (the future King George VI). Historically, Elizabeth was not alone in being a long-shot for the throne. It was only through a series of fortunate events that Elizabeth I (see no. 18) and Victoria (no. 13) became queens. For Elizabeth II, such a series of events began with the abdication of King Edward VIII in 1936, at which point her father became king, and she moved to second in line. Upon her father's death in 1952, Elizabeth became queen. She was crowned in an elaborate coronation ceremony on June 2, 1953.

Throughout her reign, Elizabeth has toured the world extensively, spoken before the United Nations and joint sessions of the U.S. Congress, and provided a steady hand at her country's helm for more than 60 years. She is already the longest-lived monarch in the United Kingdom's history. As of September 2015, she will have eclipsed Queen Victoria's record for the country's longest reign.

Though the British Empire declined in size over the years, today 16 nations and their satellites recognize Queen Elizabeth as their head of state, and most of them produce coins bearing her image. Some of the smaller nations, such as the Isle of Man, Niue, and the Cook Islands, have become the most prolific producers of Elizabethan coins in a variety of odd shapes, sizes, alloys, and colors.

The new queen, Elizabeth II, and the old symbol, Britannia, share the spotlight on this 1953 penny from Great Britain.

COLLECTING DIFFICULTY

Easy. A vast array of regular-issue, commemorative, and non-circulating legal-tender coins awaits the collector. Costs range from a few cents for modern coins of the realm to hundreds and thousands of dollars for special-issue silver and gold commemoratives.

No. 12

QUEEN ELIZABETH II

The 2006 film, The Queen, focused on the royal family's response to the death of Princess Diana (no. 6) and how Elizabeth, played by Helen Mirren, overcame negative public opinion to redeem herself in the people's hearts.

Queen Elizabeth II at NASA's Goddard Space Flight Center, circa 2007.

No. 13

QUEEN VICTORIA

Queen Victoria was the first British monarch to live in Buckingham Palace. She survived several assassination attempts, most of which involved improperly loaded guns.

The Young Queen Victoria,
by Franz Xaver Winterhalter, circa 1842.

Queen Victoria ruled the British Empire from 1837 until 1901, the longest reign of any British monarch at the time. The Victorian era became known for strict moral values, in contrast to the scandalous behavior of previous monarchs.

Victoria was born in May 1819 as Princess Alexandrina Victoria of Kent. At the time of her birth, she was fifth in line for the monarchy after her father (Prince Edward) and her three uncles (the Prince of Wales; the Duke of York; and the Duke of Clarence). King George III and Victoria's father both died in 1820, at which point her uncle became king as George IV. The Duke of York died in 1827. When George IV died in 1830, the Duke of Clarence became King William IV. Upon his death in 1837, Victoria became the new queen of England.

As heiress presumptive, Victoria considered a number of suitors as potential husbands, but her favorite was Prince Albert of Saxe-Coburg and Gotha, to whom *she* proposed in 1839 and was married in 1840. Victoria loved Prince Albert, with whom she had nine children; after his death from typhoid fever in 1861 she wore nothing but black until her own passing in 1901.

Victoria's evolution as a woman unfolds on the coins of her reign. In the early years, coins featured a so-called "young head" of Victoria, usually with her hair tied up in a bun. On the Gothic crowns of 1847 and 1853, Victoria appears in a regal pose with a full crown atop her head. For her 50-year Jubilee in 1887, she appears veiled with a small crown atop her head. In the last coins of her reign, Victoria appears heavier than in early portraits, and she wears a tiara and a veil over her hair. One of the most beautiful Victorian coins, and one of the most desired of all world coins, is the 1839 Una and the Lion 5-pound gold coin (see no. 88).

Even beyond the many coins issued during her reign, Queen Victoria remains a popular figure on coins today. Most of the countries in the British Commonwealth have issued coins with her portrait. For example, in 2013 Australia issued a colorized $1 coin to celebrate the 175th anniversary of her coronation.

This "Gothic" crown of 1847 shows a young Queen Victoria in the 10th year of her reign. This is one of the most popular of all world coin designs.

COLLECTING DIFFICULTY

Easy. The sheer quantity of many Victorian-era coins makes them affordable and easy to find. Many collectors attempt to complete date sets of the various denominations, while others collect one of each of the different types.

No. 14

SACAGAWEA

Sacagawea's son was nicknamed "Pomp" by Captain Clark, who later paid for part of his education and upbringing. No contemporary portraits exist of Sacagawea, so the coin's designer, Glenna Goodacre, used a Shoshone-Bannock woman named Randy'L He-dow Teton as her model.

Sacagawea was a young Shoshone girl who, with her husband, accompanied Meriwether Lewis, William Clark, and their Corps of Discovery in 1804 on an exploration of the Louisiana Purchase and the search for a route through the Northwest to the Pacific Ocean. Without Sacagawea's services as an interpreter and as a liaison between the white men and the Native American tribes they met, the enterprise may have failed.

The actual date and year of Sacagawea's birth remains unknown, but is believed to have been around 1788. In 1800 the Hidatsa tribe kidnapped her and sold her to a French-Canadian trapper named Toussaint Charbonneau (some accounts say he won her in a card game). Lewis and Clark hired Charbonneau as an interpreter while in Fort Mandan in North Dakota in the winter of 1804. Sacagawea, pregnant at the time, came along as his wife. In February she gave birth to their son, Jean-Baptiste Charbonneau.

Throughout the journey, Sacagawea proved to be an important member of the team, earning the special respect of Lewis and Clark. Despite illnesses, two near-drownings, and a baby on her back, Sacagawea pulled her weight. Her familiarity with the land provided valuable food in the form of berries, roots, and edible plants. Her relationship with her brother, Cameahwait, at the time the chief of the Shoshones, led to a successful negotiation for the horses they needed to complete their expedition. Her presence reassured the native tribes they met along the way that the intentions of the Corps were peaceful.

In 2000 the United States issued a new dollar coin bearing on the obverse an idealized portrait of Sacagawea with her baby son on her back. The coin's designer was Glenna Goodacre, who received as payment for her work 5,000 specially finished Sacagawea dollars; these "presentation finish" coins became very popular in the secondary market, multiplying the value of Glenna's payment by a significant factor (as of this writing they are worth at least $500 each, if not more).

Sacagawea and her infant son, called "Pomp," appear on the obverse of this gold-colored American dollar. The reverse depicts a Native American woman planting corn.

COLLECTING DIFFICULTY

Easy. The Sacagawea dollar is extremely common (though seldom used by the public because most remain stored in Treasury vaults) and inexpensive to obtain.

***Sacagawea with Lewis and Clark at Three Forks*, by Edgar Samuel Paxson.**

No. 15

ELEANOR ROOSEVELT

Eleanor stood six feet tall and considered herself an ugly duckling as a child. The Eleanor Roosevelt Monument can be seen at West 72nd Street in New York's Riverside Park. According to the Riverside Park Conservancy, this was "the first public statue of a president's wife in the nation and only the second public statue of an American woman in New York City."

Eleanor brought unprecedented activism and ability to the role of First Lady.

Eleanor Roosevelt is one of the most admired women in American history and was the leading stateswoman of her time. She authored several books, including an autobiography and a self-help book, and she wrote a syndicated newspaper column for many years. She was both outspoken and private—she championed human rights and racial equality but accepted (or overlooked) her husband's personal indiscretions.

Eleanor was born Anna Eleanor Roosevelt in October 1884. Her family was extremely wealthy. Both of her parents died before her 10th birthday, so her maternal grandmother raised her. After attending finishing school in London, Eleanor made her social debut in 1902—the same year she met her father's fifth cousin, Franklin Delano Roosevelt. She married Franklin in 1905, before he entered politics. After he was stricken with polio in 1921, Eleanor encouraged Franklin to remain in politics, and he eventually became the nation's 32nd president in 1933. Because of Franklin's three-plus terms as president, Eleanor became the longest-serving First Lady, a record that is unlikely to be exceeded because of presidential term limits put in place after Roosevelt's death.

The couple had six children, one of whom died before his first birthday. In 1918, two years after the birth of their last child, Eleanor discovered love letters between Franklin and her social secretary, Lucy Mercer. Despite her hurt, Eleanor continued to support her husband politically, but they began to live separate lives from that point on. Eleanor turned her attention to various political activities and spent much of her time traveling, giving lectures, and supporting activist causes.

After Franklin's death in 1945, Eleanor became a delegate to the United Nations General Assembly, where she championed human rights and helped draft the Universal Declaration of Human Rights in 1948.

Eleanor Roosevelt appears on a United States 2014-W First Spouse $10 gold coin as well as the associated 2014 First Spouse bronze medal. Her portraits on both feature her broad, toothy smile. Eleanor can also be seen on a variety of medals.

A jaunty-looking Eleanor Roosevelt, with her trademark, toothy grin. Her hand lights a candle on the reverse of this coin, symbolizing the light she brought to the world through her humanitarian efforts.

COLLECTING DIFFICULTY

Easy. The cost of the gold First Spouse coin can be prohibitive for some collectors, but the bronze First Spouse medal is a more reasonable alternative.

Dolley Madison was the wife of President James Madison, and the First Lady of the United States from 1809 to 1817. She was beautiful, vivacious, and entertaining, and she understood the importance of the role of First Lady in bolstering the presidency. In fact, her husband's predecessor, Thomas Jefferson, who was a widower during his term, often asked Dolley to serve as his surrogate First Lady, which she did to great effect.

She was born Dolley Payne in May 1768 in New Garden, North Carolina. In 1790 she married John Todd of Philadelphia, with whom she had two children. John and her infant son died in the yellow-fever epidemic of 1793—the same one which closed the U.S. Mint that year. Soon thereafter she met and married James Madison, then a congressman from Virginia. He retired from politics in 1797, after which the family moved to Montpelier, their plantation estate near Orange, Virginia. In 1800 Dolley and James returned to Washington when he became Jefferson's secretary of State. In 1809, when James became president, Dolley became the official First Lady.

Dolley instituted Wednesday night "drawing rooms" where upwards of 300 guests gathered in the White House to mingle with the president, the First Lady, and politicians. These events proved to be immensely successful and were held through the eight years the Madisons occupied the presidential "palace."

In 1999 the United States issued a special silver dollar to commemorate the 150th anniversary of Dolley's death. This was the first U.S. coin to honor a president's wife. In another first, the Mint allowed an outside firm, Tiffany & Co., to design the coin. Their "T & Co." initials appear on both sides. On the obverse, Cape Jasmine flowers surround a youthful bust of Dolley, which is based on a portrait by Gilbert Stuart. In the background, Mr. Madison's Temple, which rests atop an ice house at Montpelier, can be seen. On the reverse, the portico of Montpelier is shown framed by trees.

The fashionable Dolley Madison appears right at home on her Montpelier estate. Look close and you can see the Tiffany "T & Co." initials on both sides of this commemorative dollar.

COLLECTING DIFFICULTY

Easy. Both the 1999 Dolley Madison dollar and her First Spouse coin are common. The least expensive option is the bronze Dolley Madison First Spouse medal, which can be found online for less than $30.

No. 16

DOLLEY MADISON

In 1814 British forces advanced on Washington, D.C., destroying parts of the city by fire. Dolley Madison refused to leave the White House until the portrait of George Washington by Gilbert Stuart had been removed to safety.

Dolley Madison, painted by Gilbert Stuart, circa 1804.

No. 17

FLORENCE NIGHTINGALE

Florence never wore earrings. Portraits of her, especially those of her in later years, are very rare. Sir Edward Cook based his classic, two-volume biography of Florence Nightingale on her voluminous records and correspondence. In her original will, she requested that all of her records be destroyed, but she amended this instruction later and, fortunately for history, we know her much better today than we might have otherwise.

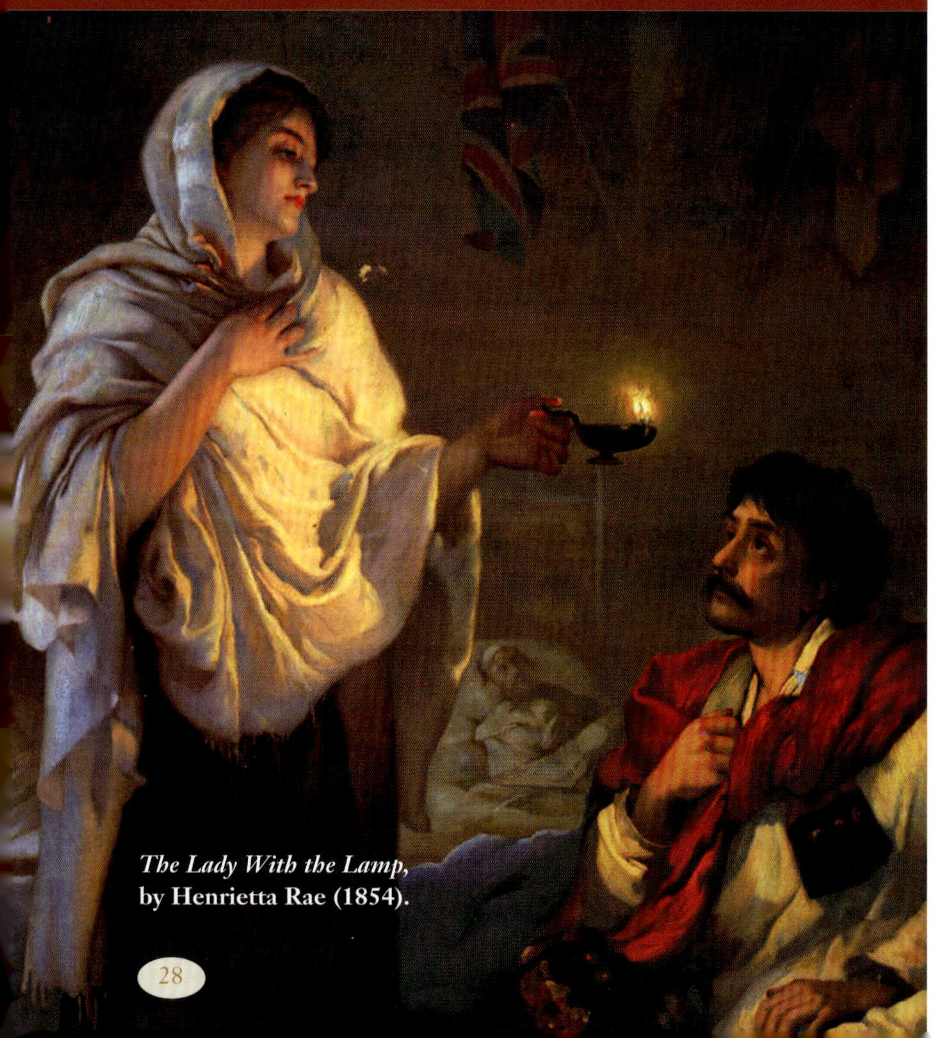

***The Lady With the Lamp*, by Henrietta Rae (1854).**

Florence Nightingale was a pioneer in nursing techniques and is known as the founder of the modern nursing profession. To feminists, she represents the emancipation of women at a time when social traditions dictated what a young girl could or could not do.

Florence was born in May 1820 to a wealthy family living in Florence, Italy. After her birth, the family moved back to England, where Florence was home-schooled by her father. She proved particularly adept at mathematics, a talent that would serve her well later in life. Her family expected her to marry and bear children, as was typical of a young woman of social standing, but she felt called to a life of service, the expression of which she found through nursing. Despite her family's objections, Florence persisted in her chosen career. In 1854, in the midst of the Crimean War, she travelled with a team of nurses to the British hospital at Scutari. There she noted the deplorable conditions and went right to work improving sanitation and hygiene, preparing food, and killing rats. Her reduction of the death rate in the military hospitals earned her praise at home in the form of poems, broadsheets, and popular songs.

Between 1851 and 1905, Florence published nearly 150 letters, books, articles, and reports of a variety of subjects ranging from nursing to pauperism to Australian aborigines to religion. In 1859 she wrote "Notes on Nursing," which became a classic textbook on nursing theory.

Florence Nightingale appears on several coins. In 2004 the tiny country of Alderney, one of the Channel Islands, issued a 5-pound coin to honor her. The reverse of the coin depicts Florence surrounded, in part, by the legend "Lady With the Lamp" (the nickname she received while making rounds late at night in the hospitals). In 2001, Gibraltar issued a one-crown Nightingale coin as part of their *Victorian Age* series.

Florence Nightingale appears as the "Lady With the Lamp" on this gold 5-pound coin from the tiny nation of Alderney, in the Channel Islands.

COLLECTING DIFFICULTY

Easy. Both the Alderney and the Gibraltar coins featuring Florence Nightingale can be found with no trouble. Both are reasonably priced, and the copper-nickel versions can be found for less than $30 each.

No. 18

QUEEN ELIZABETH I

Elizabeth I is known as the "Virgin Queen" because she never married. However, rumors of illegitimate children question the accuracy of that title. The crown jewels of Elizabeth's reign no longer exist—they were sold by Oliver Cromwell during the Commonwealth period. The crown jewels of today are replacements made in 1661.

Elizabeth I was born in September 1533 and later became the queen of England and Ireland in a reign that spanned 44 years from 1558 until her death in 1603—one of the longest reigns in England's history. However, like her later namesake, Elizabeth II (no. 12), her ascension to the throne was anything but direct.

Elizabeth's father was King Henry VIII, who divorced Catherine of Aragon to marry Elizabeth's mother, Anne Boleyn. At her birth, Elizabeth was first in line for succession, but before she was even three years old, Henry executed her mother and declared Elizabeth illegitimate. After King Henry's death in 1547, Elizabeth waited patiently as her half-brother Edward VI, the Lady Jane Grey, and her half-sister Mary each took their turns as monarchs. In 1558, at 25 years of age, Elizabeth became queen of England following Mary's death.

Elizabeth ruled by council, relying on advisors for the best course of action. She never married, though she considered several candidates, including a proposal from the Russian tsar Ivan "The Terrible."

During Elizabeth's reign, England enjoyed a lengthy period of peace and prosperity. William Shakespeare wrote many of his works in the Elizabethan era. In 1588 England won a stunning victory over the Spanish Armada, which had been sent to remove Elizabeth, known as the Protestant Queen, from the throne.

Elizabeth's position as queen ensured the placement of her portrait on the coins of England. On most Elizabethan coins, she can be seen wearing the crown of England. On silver coins, she usually holds the royal orb and scepter; on most gold coins she does not. Her elaborate dress includes the large ruff collar known as an Elizabethan collar. The largest silver denomination issued during Elizabeth's reign was the crown (roughly the size of a U.S. silver dollar). The largest gold denomination was the pound (equivalent to 20 silver shillings). Some Irish shillings bear Elizabeth's portrait on the obverse and a crowned shield with Hibernian harps on the reverse.

Elizabeth I reinforced her queenship on this undated 5-pound coin issued during her reign. Notice the high-neck ruff collar that was a frequent part of her regal attire.

COLLECTING DIFFICULTY

Moderate. Despite the comparatively large number of denominations and types bearing Elizabeth's portrait, most are scarce and expensive. Low-grade Elizabethan silver crowns run $2,000 and up; gold pounds start around $10,000.

Elizabeth I of England, painted in 1599 by Nicholas Hilliard.

No. 19

MARY TODD LINCOLN

Mary stood only five feet two inches tall. While in Springfield, Illinois, she was courted by political opponents Stephen A. Douglas and Abraham Lincoln.

Mary Todd Lincoln, circa 1846–1847.

Mary Todd Lincoln was the wife of President Abraham Lincoln. She was known for a fiery temperament but also for her grace and refinement. Though her personality differed greatly from that of her husband, she supported his political ambitions and made the best of her life in the White House, in spite of a critical media and an unwelcoming social scene. Mary suffered great loss throughout her life: her mother died when she was a young girl, and she lost three of her sons and her husband.

Mary was born Mary Ann Todd in Lexington, Kentucky, in 1818. Her father was a wealthy bank-owner and a slaveholder. In 1839 she moved to Springfield, Illinois, to live with her sister. There she met Abraham Lincoln, 10 years her senior, a lawyer and a member of the state legislature. They married, had four sons, and remained in Springfield until Lincoln became president in 1860.

Mary found life in the White House conflicting. She spent considerable amounts of money improving and redecorating the White House, for which she was criticized by the press and her husband. Because she was from Kentucky, a border state during the Civil War, and from a slave-holding family, her loyalties were questioned on all sides. Socialites in the East looked down on people from "western" states (as Kentucky was called), and thus Mary had a hard time fitting into the elite society of Washington, D.C.

Following the assassination of her husband in April 1865, Mary was grief-stricken. She became depressed, and her behaviors became odd and sometimes self-destructive, leading her son, Robert, to commit her to a mental institution. She was only 63 years old when she died in 1882.

In 2010 the United States issued a gold $10 First Spouse coin honoring Mary Todd Lincoln. The portrait on the obverse matches that of a photograph of Mary taken by Matthew Brady in 1862. The reverse shows her bringing flowers to injured soldiers, a duty she performed as First Lady. In 2003 Liberia struck a $20 coin featuring Mary Lincoln as part of its *America's First Lady* series.

On the obverse of this First Spouse coin, Mary Todd Lincoln wears a floral headdress. On the reverse, she is shown delivering flowers to convalescing soldiers during the Civil War.

COLLECTING DIFFICULTY

Easy. Mary's First Spouse coins and medals are readily available. Her First Spouse medal is an attractive, affordable option.

No. 20

THE STATUE OF LIBERTY

The Statue of Liberty is a revised version of a similar design for a lighthouse proposed by Bartholdi in 1869 for the entrance to the Suez Canal. The French engineer Gustave Eiffel, who later created the Paris tower that bears his name, designed the interior support system for the Statue of Liberty.

The Statue of Liberty (originally known as "Liberty Enlightening the World") is one of the most famous and recognizable of all American landmarks. Each year millions of visitors take the ferry ride from New York to Liberty Island to enjoy this historic monument. For the many European immigrants who came to America by boat in the late 1800s and early 1900s, the Statue of Liberty was a poignant first impression of their new home.

Though often described as a gift from France, the Statue of Liberty was the result of fundraising efforts on both sides of the Atlantic. The people of France raised money for the privately produced statue, and the Americans raised money for the pedestal. Fundraising proved difficult at times, and the lack of finances caused numerous delays in the project. Many famous people promoted the statue, including the poet Emma Lazarus, whose "The New Colossus" included the now-famous lines, "Give me your tired, your poor, your huddled masses...."

Designed by French sculptor Frédéric Auguste Bartholdi, the Statue of Liberty consists of pre-formed copper plates attached to a steel structure. In 1876 Bartholdi raised money for the construction of the statue by charging admission to view Liberty's torch hand at the Philadelphia Centennial Celebration. The Statue of Liberty was completed and dedicated in 1886.

In 1986 the United States issued a half dollar, a silver dollar, and a gold $5 coin to commemorate the centennial of the Statue of Liberty. In 1997 the U.S. Mint began marketing "American Eagle" platinum bullion coins in a variety of sizes and denominations, each showing a close-up view of the Statue's head. The one-ounce Proof coins are the most interesting, as each year features a new reverse design, always with an eagle on display either prominently or subtly. The 2001 State quarter from New York features a Statue of Liberty imposed on a silhouette of the state. Other countries, including France and Liberia, have issued coins depicting the Statue of Liberty.

The Statue of Liberty enlightens the world from her pedestal on Liberty Island. The reverse of this coin shows a family of immigrants, fresh off the boat in their new American home.

COLLECTING DIFFICULTY

Easy. The 1986 Statue of Liberty commemorative half dollars are relatively inexpensive and easy to obtain for less than $10. All of the platinum issues boast low mintages and high prices because of their intrinsic metal value.

The Statue of Liberty stands tall.

No. 21

ABIGAIL ADAMS

Gilbert Stuart began his painting of Abigail in 1800, when she was 56 years old. For some reason, he did not deliver her portrait, or that of her husband, until 1815, well after they had left the White House.

Abigail Adams was the wife of John Adams, second president of the United States. She was also the mother of John Quincy Adams, the sixth president. Thanks to a voluminous correspondence between her and her husband, modern historians know more about Abigail than many other First Ladies, many of whom left no such treasure troves of information. The 2008 television mini-series, *John Adams*, introduced Abigail to millions of viewers.

Abigail Smith was born in November 1744 in Weymouth in the Province of Massachusetts (then a British colony). Her mother, Elizabeth, taught sickly Abigail at home, taking advantage of the large family library. Despite the lack of a formal education, Abigail became quite the intellectual.

In 1764 Abigail married John Adams, her third cousin, who at the time was a country lawyer. Beginning in 1788, John was sent to Europe on a series of diplomatic missions, which took him away from Abigail and his family. Nevertheless, she joined him in France from 1784 to 1785. In 1796 John became president and the family moved to Philadelphia, which was the nation's capital while the White House was being constructed. Abigail took an active role as First Lady, overseeing formal dinners at the presidential mansion in Philadelphia. In 1800 John and Abigail became the first residents of the White House.

In 2007 the United States produced a gold $10 First Spouse coin for Abigail. The portrait on the obverse was taken from a painting done by Gilbert Stuart. The reverse of the coin shows a young Abigail gathering her thoughts about what to write with her quill pen. The legend "Remember the Ladies" refers to a quote from a letter she wrote to her husband in 1776, in which she asked her husband to treat women favorably in the laws of the new nation. As a companion piece to the First Spouse coin, the U.S. Mint made a bronze First Spouse medal, which has a similar design but fewer legends.

On her First Spouse coin of 2007, Abigail Adams implores her husband to "Remember the Ladies" when creating the new laws for America. Unfortunately for the ladies, he did not.

Lithograph of Abigail Adams, circa 1900.

COLLECTING DIFFICULTY

Easy. The Abigail Adams First Spouse coin is plentiful but can be expensive because it contains half an ounce of gold. For the average collector, her bronze First Spouse medal is the more affordable alternative.

No. 22

GRACE KELLY

After Princess Grace accepted Prince Rainier's marriage proposal, he informed her that she must bring a dowry of $2 million to the marriage, which she did.

Grace Kelly was an American actress and, later, the princess of Monaco. She was known for her exceptional beauty and sense of style. In 1982 her life was cut short after a tragic car accident.

Grace was born Grace Patricia Kelly in 1929 in Philadelphia. As a young girl, she developed a love for acting and appeared in her first play at the age of 12. She acted and danced in high school, then left home to pursue an acting career in New York. She worked as a model to support herself and eventually found roles in plays, theaters, and on television. Her first big break came in 1949 when she performed in the Broadway play *The Father*. Her first film role was in *Fourteen Hours*, followed by her breakout role in the 1952 film *High Noon*, where she starred as Gary Cooper's wife. Numerous film roles followed in which she worked with Clark Gable (*Magombo*), Ray Milland (*Dial M For Murder*), Jimmy Stewart (*Rear Window*), and William Holden and Bing Crosby (*Country Girl*). She won an Oscar for Best Actress for her work in *Country Girl*.

In 1955 Grace attended the Cannes Film Festival, where, on a side trip to Monaco, she met Prince Rainier III. They married in April 1956 in a fairy-tale wedding attended by thousands. The couple had three children: Princess Caroline, Prince Albert, and Princess Stephanie. On September 13, 1982, Grace died from injuries sustained in an accident, on her way to Monaco, in which she lost control of her car and plunged down a mountainside.

Princess Grace can be seen on several coins. In 1966 the London firm of Spink and Sons commissioned the Paris Mint to strike 10- and 200-franc coins to commemorate the 10th anniversary of Prince Rainier and Grace's marriage. In 1982, following Grace's death, Monaco produced a coin with a profile portrait of Grace on the obverse and a large rose on the reverse. In 1996 Gibraltar issued a crown honoring Grace as part of their *Centenary of Cinema* series. On the 25th anniversary of Grace's death in 2007, Monaco produced a bi-metallic 2-euro coin.

Grace Kelly and Prince Rainier III appear on a 200-franc gold coin of Monaco. Even though Grace's head is in the dominant, foreground position, it is oddly tiny.

COLLECTING DIFFICULTY

Easy. Grace Kelly coins range in price from inexpensive to pricey. The 2007 Monaco 2-euro coin turned out to be a runaway hit—the mintage of 20,000 pieces is low, but not unusually so. Nevertheless, the price in online offerings as of this publication is around $2,000, nearly twice the current catalog value.

Grace Kelly departing New York on her way to Monaco for her wedding to Prince Rainier.

No. 23

NIKE

After his victory over Mark Antony, the emperor Octavian built an altar to Victory featuring a golden statue of the goddess Nike that had been captured nearly 300 years before. Unfortunately, the statue no longer exists.

Statue of the goddess Nike.

Nike was a member of the Greek pantheon of gods and goddesses. Her mother was the river-goddess Styx; her father was Pallas, one of the Titans. Her siblings included Zelos, Kratos, and Bia, all of whom joined Nike and their mother as allies of Zeus in his war against the Titans. Nike is most often portrayed as driving a chariot or as a small winged figure presenting a crown of laurel to victors in battles or games. On Greek coins, she is shown in a variety of similar styles or standing on the hand of the goddess Athena, with whom she is often associated. In Roman mythology, Nike became the goddess Victory (or Victoria).

Nike was a favored and frequent theme in Greek art and sculpture. The winged Nike of Samothrace, currently housed in the Louvre Museum in Paris, represents one of the finest expressions of Greek sculpture. Though missing a head, a wing, a breast, and both arms, the statue captures the movement of wind across Nike's wings and the drapery of her robe as she stood on the prow of a ship during a sea battle.

How the Nike of Samothrace held her arms and hands is the subject of fanciful speculation. Perhaps a clue can be found on some of the coins from around the time the statue existed. Several Macedonian tetradrachms depict Nike advancing on a prow, just as she does on the statue. In one case, Nike blows a long trumpet supported by her right hand as she cradles a stylis (staff) in her left arm.

The United States issued a $5 gold coin for the 1988 Olympics with a head of Nike wearing a headband that reads "In God We Trust." This was an odd conflation of a Greek goddess with a motto intended for the Judeo-Christian God.

A confusing pairing of the goddess Nike with the motto "In God We Trust." Should we trust goddess or God?

COLLECTING DIFFICULTY

Moderate. Greek coins depicting Nike and Roman coins depicting Victory range from common and inexpensive to rare and valuable. Numerous, low-grade examples can be found online starting around $100. Better-quality examples can be found in international auctions at higher prices.

No. 24

Queen Nefertiti

Queen Nefertiti's tomb has never been found. The left eye of Nefertiti's bust lacks the quartz iris seen in the right eye. Despite an intensive search at the time the bust was discovered, the missing piece was never found.

Nefertiti was queen of Egypt during the 18th dynasty (14th century BC). She was the wife of Pharoah Akhenaten, who was notorious for initiating a monotheistic religion that worshipped only one god, Aten. Akhenaten is famous for being the father of King Tut (Tutankhamen), thus making Nefertiti either Tut's mother or his aunt (the relationship is unclear).

There are two aspects to Queen Neferiti's story. The first is her place in the Egyptian historical record. The second is the famous bust of Nefertiti, discovered in Egypt early in the 20th century.

Nefertiti appears in a variety of hieroglyphic scenes in both Thebes and later in Akhetaten (now Amarna), after Akhenaten moved the capital there. Over a 10- or 11-year period, Nefertiti bore six children with Akhenaten, including the future wife of Tutankhamen. In one surviving scene, Nefertiti and Akhenaten play with three of their daughters—the odd shape of their heads has given rise to the theory that the ancient Egyptians came from a race of aliens.

The bust of Nefertiti is one of the most famous and celebrated works of Egyptian art. In 1912 the German archaeologist Ludwig Borchardt found the bust in a workshop in Amarna, Egypt, attributed to Thutmose. The bust is made of limestone layered in painted stucco. In 1913 Borchardt and the Egyptian government split his finds 50-50 in a negotiated deal. Egypt maintains today that Borchardt duped them by understating the value of the Nefertiti bust and hiding it from the inspector responsible for determining the split. The fact that Borchardt kept the bust hidden until 1920 didn't help matters. Once the Egyptian government learned of the Nefertiti bust's existence, they demanded its return, a claim they continue to pursue.

Queen Nefertiti appears on numerous coins, invariably in the form of the Thutmose bust. In 1994 Egypt issued a silver 5-pound coin and a gold 50-pound coin with the bust of Nefertiti in a plain field. Fiji, Belarus, the British Virgin Islands, the Cook Islands, and the Solomon Islands have all issued Nefertiti coins.

Queen Nefertiti appears on the obverse of this 1994 Egyptian 50-pound gold coin. This is a perfect likeness of the statue of Nefertiti, one of the most famous of all Egyptian archaeological finds.

COLLECTING DIFFICULTY

Easy. Collectors have several options, most of which are inexpensive and can be located readily. Nefertiti coins come in a variety of shapes, sizes, and metals. One of the more interesting pieces is the Belarus 20-ruble rectangular coin, the obverse of which features the Thutmose bust and the reverse of which shows a hieroglyph of Nefertiti's husband, Akhenaten, holding one of their children.

Bust of Queen Nefertiti in the Neues Museum, Berlin.

No. 25

BRITANNIA AND MARIANNE

Great Britain and France were not always good friends. For example, during the Revolutionary War, America relied heavily on France to help defeat the British. The *Entente Cordiale* ended hundreds of years of strained relations between the two countries.

National Service by Septimus E. Scott. Poster for the National Service Industrial Army, showing Britannia with the Union Jack.

Hero land, or, over the top with Uncle Sam and his allies. Poster for a fundraising event showing Marianne bearing a sword and shield.

At times, both Great Britain and France have chosen allegorical female figures to represent their respective countries. In France, Marianne represents liberty and republican ideals as replacements for the self-indulgence of the former kings. In Great Britain, Britannia supplements the monarchy and presents a personification of the British people.

Britannia first appeared on British pattern coins in 1665 and on regular-issue coins in 1672. She appeared on copper coins throughout the 17th, the 18th, and most of the 19th centuries. In 1895 she began appearing on the British trade dollar, which was intended for use in the Orient. Nowadays, Britannia can be seen in various forms only on the silver and gold bullion coins that bear her name.

Marianne is a more recent invention, as she did not arise until the French Revolution. Her first appearance on a French coin was in Year 4 (1795) of the First Republic. She faced left and wore the distinctive Phrygian cap, representing freedom from slavery. Her appearance on French coins was short-lived; as soon as Napoleon became First Consul, the coins returned to the male-dominated, monarchial themes of the past. A new female figure graced French coins beginning in 1870, but the old Marianne, with her Phrygian cap, did not reappear until 1898. Since then Marianne has appeared in a variety of forms and styles on French coins.

In 2004 Great Britain issued a special 5-pound coin in both copper-nickel and silver to celebrate the 100th anniversary of the *Entente Cordiale*, an alliance signed between Great Britain and France to counter German expansion. The reverse of the coin features Britannia and Marianne in an unusual, upside-down, right-side-up arrangement. Thus, British subjects will prefer Britannia in the right-side-up position, and the French will orient Marianne right-side-up. In 2004 France issued silver coins denominated as one-and-a-half euros and gold 20-euro coins with an identical reverse. These were two rare occurrences of the national symbols of two different nations appearing on the same coin.

Britannia and Marianne appear together on this topsy-turvy 5-pound coin of Great Britain. France issued nearly identical coins to celebrate the 100th anniversary of the historic *Entente Cordiale* agreement between the two countries.

COLLECTING DIFFICULTY

Easy. Both the British 5-pound coins and the French coins denominated as one-and-a-half euros are easy to locate for less than $100. The French 20-euro coin is a trifle more elusive and much more expensive because of its tiny mintage of only 339 pieces.

No. 26

FEMALE ATHLETE

The number of women athletes on coins has increased over the years, as has their proportion relative to male athletes.

Female athletes on coins are a relatively new phenomenon in the sense that the appearance of such issues has occurred only in the past 40 or 50 years. The first circulating Olympic coins of the modern era appeared in 1951 when Finland issued a 500-markkaa silver coin to commemorate the 1952 Helsinki games. Even then, no athletes appeared on the coins—only the Olympic rings. In 1968 Mexico issued a 25-peso Olympic coin with the first athlete—a male Aztecan playing *ullamaliztli*.

The first female athlete appeared on a modern coin in 1972, when West Germany issued a series of silver 10 marks to commemorate the Munich Olympics. The female appeared on the *Athletes* series as a nude; she holds either a pole for the vault or a paddle for canoeing. In 1976 Canada issued $5 commemorative coins for their Montreal Olympics, one featuring a female javelin thrower, another a female platform diver, and a third a female shot-putter. In preparation for the 1980 Moscow Olympics, Russia issued a series of 5- and 10-rouble commemorative coins, most with male athletes, but one with a female gymnast and another with a female archer. In 1984 the United States issued a $10 gold Olympic commemorative coin with a female torch-runner on the obverse (along with her male counterpart). The South Korean coins for the 1988 Seoul Olympics favored male athletes but included a higher percentage of female athletes—as handball, volleyball, and badminton players, a high diver, a gymnast, and (curiously) elaborately dressed girls on a swing. In 1988 East Germany issued a 10-mark coin to commemorate their nation's sports, this time with an all-female cast of three runners.

While most female athletes on coins tend to be allegorical figures, a few countries have honored real women such as Martina Navratilova and Chris Evert.

With careful searching, almost any sport in which females participate can be found on a coin. From hurdlers to sprinters to ribbon dancers (rhythmic gymnasts) and just about everything in between, some country will have created a coin for that sport.

The first coin of the modern era to feature a female athlete was this German 10-mark coin issued for the 1972 Olympics.

COLLECTING DIFFICULTY

Easy and inexpensive. A collection of coins featuring female athletes and their various sports can be a specialty all by itself and can be as small or as large as the collector desires.

A female pole-vaulter stands at the ready.

No. 27

ATHENA/ MINERVA

Athens received its name as the result of a contest between Athena and Poseidon for naming rights. In one version of the story, the citizens of the city voted for either Athena or Poseidon, resulting in a one-vote victory for Athena. In another version, Athena and Poseidon presented gifts to the citizens to win their favor. The people chose Athena's gift—the olive tree.

***Pallas Athena*, by Gustav Klimt, circa 1898.**

Athena is one of the most famous of all the Greek goddesses. She is known most commonly as the virgin goddess of wisdom. The myths of Athena are many and vary over time based on cultural changes. She survived into Roman times as the goddess Minerva.

Athena was the daughter of Zeus and the Titan goddess Metis, also representative of wisdom. Athena's birth was anything but normal. It seems that Zeus convinced Metis to turn herself into a fly, and then he swallowed her to prevent her from bearing children that might become a threat. However, Metis was already pregnant, and, while in Zeus's belly, she forged armor for her daughter Athena. Hephaestus, the blacksmith of the gods, struck Zeus's head, cracking it open, and out jumped Athena, fully grown and armored.

The Greeks revered Athena, naming Athens after her and erecting the Parthenon temple for her on the Acropolis (*parthenos* means "virgin" in Greek). She is most often associated with the owl, and it is from her that the owl has gained its reputation for wisdom.

Athena appeared on ancient Greek coins over several centuries, from around the sixth to the second century BC; then on Roman coins from the second century BC until well into the second century AD. She is shown in a variety of poses. On the obverse of Greek coins, she usually appears wearing a helmet of some sort (remember, she was born with armor). The reverses of the earliest types feature an owl; occasionally, a bull or pegasus appears. Sometimes the reverse depicts a full-length Nike. On later coins, Athena is shown seated on a throne with a tiny Nike in her outstretched hand (see no. 80). In Roman times, Minerva is usually relegated to the reverse of coins, where she is often shown as a standing figure.

In modern times, Athena/Minerva can be found on coins from a variety of places: Austria; the German state of Bamberg; Gibraltar; Greece; Sweden; the United States; and others.

An early, somewhat crude portrait of Athena appears on the obverse of this silver tetradrachm of Attica/Athens from between 454 and 404 BC. The reverse shows a small, bug-eyed owl.

COLLECTING DIFFICULTY

Easy. Numerous ancient silver and gold coins bear Athena's portrait, and many are reasonably priced. Modern coins are even more affordable and accessible. Athena-themed coins would make a relatively large collection that would include different portraits and a variety of different reverse designs.

No. 28

VENUS DE MILO

The Venus de Milo is one of the most famous and instantly recognizable statues from Ancient Greece. Millions of visitors each year flock to the statue in its present place in the Louvre Museum in Paris, France. Made of joined blocks of white marble, the statue depicts the Greek goddess Aphrodite (Venus to the Romans). The statue is named after the island of Melos, where it was discovered in 1820. Several pieces are missing from the statue, including both of her arms and part of the plinth (base) on which she stands.

As is often the case, background stories can be as fascinating as their subjects. The story of the Venus de Milo includes myths, misinformation, and politics. The statue was found on the Greek island of Melos in early 1820 by either a farmer plowing his field or a peasant who uncovered an ancient shrine. When discovered, both of the arms were intact: the outstretched left arm held an apple in its hand, while the right arm protected the drapery from falling. Supposedly, sailors arguing over possession of the statue dragged it across rocks and broke off both arms. In fact, fragments of her left arms and hand, as well as a piece broken off of the plinth, were found with the statue. At first, the piece of the plinth was discredited, though it fit perfectly, because it indicated a lesser-known sculptor and a date from a period in which such quality work was unknown.

The Venus de Milo appears on coins of France and Costa Rica. In 1993 France issued a 100-franc silver coin to commemorate the 200th anniversary of the Louvre Museum. Of all the magnificent works contained in the Louvre, which piece of art did they choose to represent the museum? The answer is, of course, the Venus de Milo. The Costa Rican 20-colón coin of 1970 features a nice, full-length image of the statue. Some Mardi Gras tokens, given out as colorful festival souvenirs in New Orleans, feature the Venus de Milo.

This French 100-franc silver coin presents a high-quality portrait of the Venus de Milo. The reverse of the coin shows the unusual glass pyramid structures in front of the Louvre Museum, where the Venus de Milo "lives."

COLLECTING DIFFICULTY

Easy. The 1993 French 100-franc coin appears occasionally in online auctions and direct sales. The Costa Rican coin is a bit more elusive and expensive; it can appear as an individual coin or as part of the 1970 Proof set.

In May 1920, Robert Aitken, designer of the 1915 Panama-Pacific $50 gold coins, the 1921 Missouri Centennial half dollar, and the 1925 California Diamond Jubilee half dollar, criticized the way in which the Louvre presented the Venus de Milo. He disagreed with the way the lighting hit the statue, arguing that no sculptor had ever been consulted in the best way to display the Venus.

The Venus de Milo is located in the Louvre in Paris, France.

No. 29

THE BRONTË SISTERS

In 1848, to dispel rumors that their novels were the work of a single writer, Charlotte and Anne visited their London publishers to prove that the three sisters were, in fact, the authors. In their lifetime, the three sisters never published under their actual names.

The Brontë Sisters, **by Patrick Branwell Brontë, a digital restoration of the original painting.**

The Brontë sisters, Anne, Emily, and Charlotte, were literary giants from the 1800s.

Charlotte Brontë was born in April 1816 in the small town of Thornton in West Yorkshire, England (also the birthplace of Emily and Anne). She wrote poems and four novels, including *Jane Eyre*. She died in 1855 at the age of 38.

Emily Jane Brontë was born in July 1818. She wrote poems and only one novel, *Wuthering Heights*. She died in 1848 at the age of 30.

Anne Brontë was born in January 1820. She wrote poems and the novels *Agnes Grey* and *The Tenant of Wildfell Hall*. She died in 1848 at the age of 29.

Their first work was a collection of poetry published in 1846, entitled simply "Poems." The sisters wrote under male pseudonyms because of the difficulty of getting works by female authors published. Charlotte became "Currer," Emily became "Ellis," Anne became "Acton," and their last name, Brontë, became "Bell."

In 1847 all three sister published novels using their masculine pseudonyms. Charlotte wrote *Jane Eyre*, which became an instant success. Emily wrote *Wuthering Heights*, and Anne wrote *Agnes Grey*. Reviewers suspected that the authors of these novels were women, but the sisters maintained their cover.

Following the death of her sisters in 1848, Charlotte continued to write novels as Currer Bell, publishing *Shirley* in 1849 and *Villette* in 1853. In 1857, two years after her death, her first book, *The Professor*, written before *Jane Eyre*, was finally published.

In 2001 Gibraltar issued a Brontë sisters coin as part of their *The Victorian Age* series. The obverse of the coin features a bust of Queen Elizabeth II; the reverse features Anne, Emily, and Charlotte. Their portraits were taken from a painting of the sisters done around 1834 by their brother, Branwell.

Three of the greatest authors of the Victorian era, Anne, Emily, and Charlotte Brontë appear together on this 2001 crown of Gibraltar.

COLLECTING DIFFICULTY

Easy. The Gibraltar crown is inexpensive and easy to find. It is the only coin that shows all three sisters together.

No. 30

CLEOPATRA THEA

On coins, Thea always took the foreground, the position of honor, when she appeared with another person, even when it was with her husband, King Balas.

Cleopatra Thea was one of numerous Egyptian Cleopatras, but she is not nearly as famous as Cleopatra VII (no. 4, who was also known, confusingly, as *Thea Philopator*). Her name means Cleopatra the Goddess, though she was completely mortal. She was born around 164 to Ptolemy VI and Cleopatra II. Very little is known of her early life, but she eventually came to rule Syria. She was an incredibly ambitious woman who was unafraid to kill to achieve her ends.

The first of Thea's three husbands was Alexander Balas, ruler of the Seleucid Kingdom, which covered a wide swath of the Middle East, from Turkey in the west through most of the area occupied by modern-day Syria, Iraq, Iran, and Afghanistan. Balas died fighting Demetrius II Nicator of Syria. Cleopatra then married Demetrius and remained with him until the Parthians took him into captivity. With Demetrius away, Cleopatra married his younger brother, Antiochus VII of Sidon. In 129 BC, the Parthians released Demetrius, allowing him to reclaim his throne and his wife. Three years later, after Demetrius's defeat at Damascus, Cleopatra barred him from the city, and he was tortured and killed. His oldest son, Seleucus, became king. Cleopatra quickly had him murdered so she could reign as coruler with her son, Antiochus VIII. When Antiochus proved uncooperative, Cleopatra attempted to murder him with poisoned wine, but he turned the tables on her by making her drink it instead. Cleopatra Thea died—of poisoning—in 121 BC.

Cleopatra Thea is found on coins of the Seleucid Empire in a conjoined portrait with her husband, Alexander Balas. Occasionally, Thea is seen wearing a mural crown in the fashion of the Greek goddess Tyche. Thea can also be seen on coins with her son, Antiochus VIII Grypus. There, she wears a stephane (decorative headband) and a veil.

Cleopatra appears with her son Antiochus VIII on the obverse of this Seleucid Kingdom tetradrachm of 122–121 BC. This was the same son she tried to poison.

COLLECTING DIFFICULTY

Moderate. Bronze coins bearing Cleopatra Thea's image are the most affordable options available to collectors; they can be found from $250 to $350. Silver coins are more expensive and start around $800. Certain "Thea" types can run into the thousands of dollars.

A modern conception of Cleopatra Thea, by Barry Brown Jr.

No. 31

MARIE CURIE

Marie was almost excluded from the nomination for the Nobel Prize for Physics because she was a woman. However, a committee member alerted Pierre, who insisted that she be included in the nomination. Marie's daughter, Irene, went on to win a Nobel Prize of her own.

Marie Sklodowska Curie was a pioneer both in scientific exploration and in the realm of female representation in science.

Marie Curie was a Polish-born scientist who won two Nobel prizes for her groundbreaking work in radioactivity and chemistry. She became world famous after winning the Nobel Prize in 1903. She and her husband published numerous papers based on their research, and Marie won numerous accolades as a scientist.

Marie was born Maria Salomea Sklodowska in Warsaw, Poland, in November 1867. While she was a young girl, her family experienced financial difficulties, and Marie lost a sister and her mother before the age of 10. She excelled in school, winning a gold medal upon graduation from a *gymnasium* in 1883. In place of college, which was closed to women at the time, Marie read books, hired tutors, and attended the underground Flying University. In 1891 she left for Paris, where she entered the University of Paris to begin her studies. She earned a degree in physics in 1893. She then went on to earn a second degree in 1894. She met her future husband, Pierre Curie, also a scientist, and the couple married in 1895.

In 1898 Marie and Pierre discovered the radioactive element polonium, named by Marie after her native country. The pair also discovered radium. In 1903 Marie finally earned her doctorate and won the Nobel Prize for Physics, sharing it with her husband and Henri Becquerel.

Marie lost her husband, Pierre, in 1906, when he was crushed by a wagon while crossing a street. In 1934 Marie died of aplastic anemia resulting from her improper handling of radioactive material throughout her career.

Marie Curie appears on several coins from Poland, her native homeland, and France, her adopted home. In 1967 she was featured on a Polish 10-zlotych coin to commemorate the centennial of her birth. In 1974 Poland issued a 100-zlotych coin to honor Marie and her discovery of radium. A 1998 Polish 20-zlotych coin commemorated the 100th anniversary of the discovery of radium and polonium; the reverse of the coins shows Marie and Pierre at work, as well as the symbols of *Po* and *Ra* in large letters.

This Polish 100-zlotych coin from 1974 shows a stylized bust of Marie Curie facing left, with the symbol *Ra* (for radium) in the right field.

COLLECTING DIFFICULTY

Easy. An online search for Marie Curie coins revealed at least six options ranging in price from a mere $2 to $2,750. A nice mini-collection of Marie Curie coins can be assembled at a reasonable cost.

No. 32

VIRGINIA DARE

The world rarely notices when people are born ... after all, there are so many of them. However, when a young girl was born on August 18, 1587, in the Roanoke colony, she became the first white child born in America to English parents. Her name was Virginia and she was the daughter of Ananias and Eleanor Dare. Her grandfather, John White, was the governor of the colony. John left for England a few months after Virginia's birth but was delayed from returning because of the Anglo-Spanish War. When he finally arrived at the colony in 1590, all of the settlers, including Virginia, were gone, with no clue as to their whereabouts.

What happened to Virginia and the rest of the colonists? Did they perish of disease or malnutrition? Did local Indians kill or kidnap them? Without hard facts, one can only speculate. In his novel *White Seed: The Untold Story of the Lost Colony of Roanoke*, author Paul Clayton created a scenario where the colonists faced two threats: from the hostile Chief Powhatan; and from a power-mad soldier within the colony itself. In the end, the heroine of the book, Maggie, escaped with friendly Indians, taking Eleanor and Virginia with her; the rest of the colony was slaughtered. When Captain White returned with a resupply ship and searched for the colonists, Maggie deliberately avoided him, fearing having to return to England. White believed he heard the cry of a child (Virginia), which haunted him as he returned to sea.

In 1937 the United States issued a half dollar to commemorate the 350th anniversary of the colonization of Roanoke Island and the birth of Virginia Dare. The obverse of the coin features a profile bust of Sir Walter Raleigh, the original receiver of the colony's charter. The reverse of the coin shows Eleanor Dare holding her newborn baby girl, Virginia. Two ships flank Eleanor.

Eleanor Dare cradles her baby daughter, Virginia, on this special half dollar commemorating the founding of the ill-fated Roanoke Colony. No one knows what became of Eleanor and Virginia.

COLLECTING DIFFICULTY

Easy. The 1937 Roanoke half dollar is common and reasonably priced at $200 to $300 in Mint State.

Of the 100 Greatest Women on Coins, Virginia appears as the tiniest—in terms of both age and size. Brenau University in Gainesville, Georgia, holds a number of "Dare Stones," which bear inscriptions supposedly left by Eleanor Dare describing what befell the colony. Most were found 400 to 500 miles from Roanoke near Gainesville and Atlanta, and the authenticity of the stones has been hotly debated.

***The Baptism of Virginia Dare*, by Henry Howe, circa 1876.**

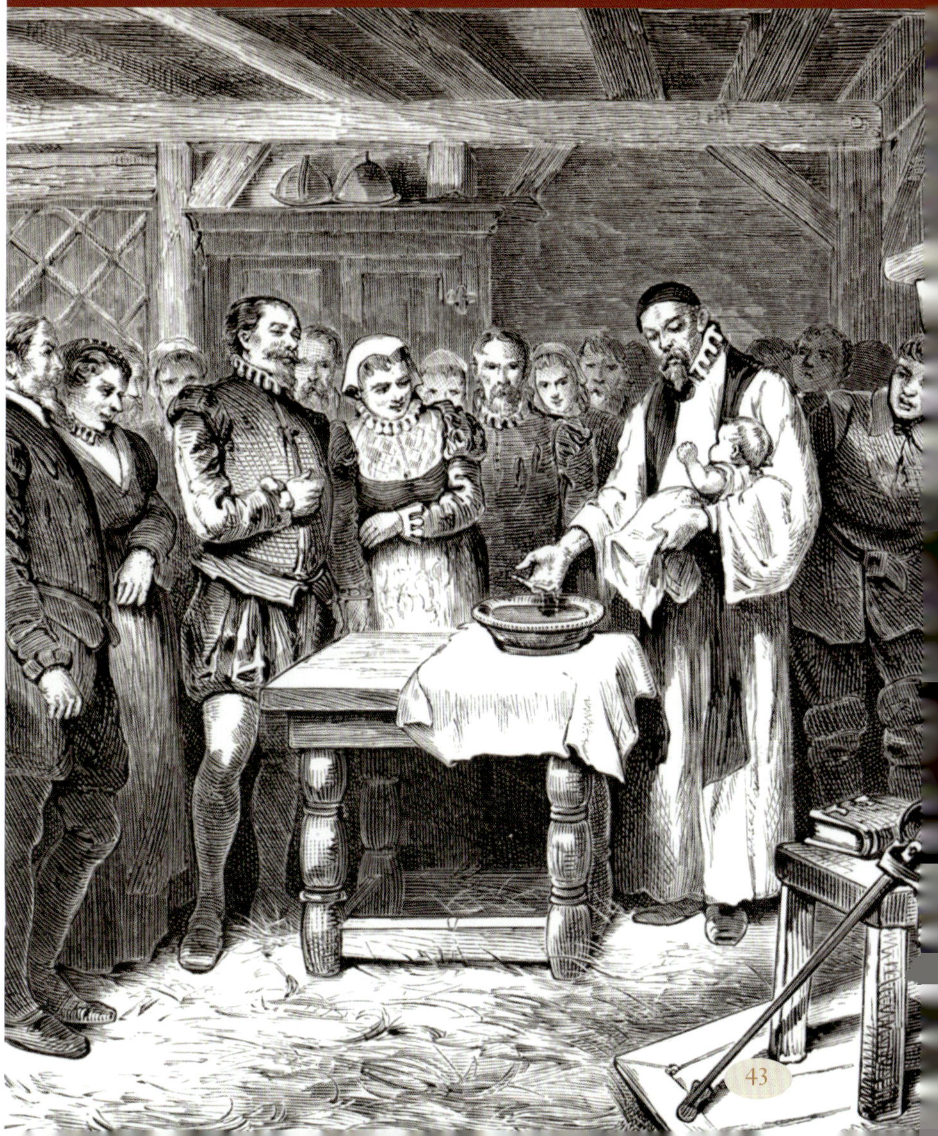

No. 33

MYTHOLOGICAL MOTHER EARTH

When Cronos castrated Uranus, the latter's testicles fell into the sea. From them arose the goddess Aphrodite.

Sarcophagus with Mother Earth adorning the side.

In Greek mythology, Gaia (Earth) is literally the mother of everything. In essence, she is the "big bang" theory of the Greeks. The Gaia story is outlandish and shocking, but it gave the Greeks a way to explain the creation of the Earth and everything around them. The following is based on Hesiod's *Theogony*; other accounts, such as those by Homer and Virgil, vary.

Before Gaia, there was nothing, not even Time, only Chaos. To overcome her loneliness, Gaia created a son, Uranus (Heaven, or Sky), with whom she mated and subsequently gave birth to the Titans. Uranus became jealous of Gaia's children, forcing her to hide them from his wrath. To protect them, she created a new element—adamantine (or gray adamant)—and fashioned a sickle out of it. This she gave to her son, Cronos (Time), and the next time Uranus attempted to mate with her, Cronos castrated him. The blood of Uranus impregnated Gaia, leading to the birth of the Erinyes, the Giants, and the Meliae (forerunners of the human race). Gaia had other children with Uranus, including the Cyclopes and the Hecatonchires (who each had 50 heads and 100 arms). She also mated with her son Pontus to create the sea gods.

From two of the Titans, Cronos and Rhea, came the 12 Greek gods, including Zeus, Hera, Ares, Hades, Poseidon, Demeter, and other gods less familiar. From Zeus came Athena, Hermes, Apollo, Artemis, and Dionysus.

In Roman mythology, Gaia is Tellus or Terra, the Latin word for Earth.

In 1994 the Marshall Islands produced a set of 12 brass coins as part of their *Wonders of the Solar System* series. The obverse of the coins features the official seal of the Marshall Islands. The reverse shows a mythological Mother Earth with a child on her lap. The zodiac symbol for Earth is in the foreground, giving the impression that Earth is riding in a wheelchair or some wheel-driven vehicle. Several Roman coins and medallions show Tellus reclining on the reverse, often with her hand on a globe.

Mother Earth reclines on the reverse of this bronze Roman sestertius from the period between 117 and 138 AD. Her right hand rests on a globe. Her name, Tellvstarii (Tellus), appears at upper right.

COLLECTING DIFFICULTY

Moderate. The Marshall Islands 1994 $10 coins were sold as part of a set of 12 pieces, and because most of the sets remain intact, finding the individual Mother Earth coin is difficult. However, the complete set does include another female: Venus. Roman coins and medallions depicting Tellus are scarce, hard to find, and expensive.

No. 34

EMPRESS MARIA THERESA OF AUSTRIA

Following Maria's death, the Austrian Mint began producing restrikes of the 1780 Maria Theresa taler. According to the Austrian Mint's Web site (www.muenzeoesterreich.at), the Maria Theresa taler has been produced continuously since 1857.

Maria Theresa ruled the Austrian Empire for 40 years, between 1740 and 1780. As a woman, she was barred from becoming the Holy Roman Emperor following her father's death, but she became Holy Roman Empress as a result of her marriage to Francis I. Though not the emperor in name, Maria wielded considerable power: first through her husband, and then through two of her sons until her death in 1780.

In May 1717, Maria entered the world as Archduchess Maria Theresa Walburga Amalia Christina, the daughter of the Holy Roman Emperor Charles VI and Elisabeth Christine of the German duchy of Brunswick-Wolfenbuttel. She married Francis Stephen of Lorraine in 1736 and subsequently bore him 16 children in less than 20 years. Several of her children went on to become powerful in their own right: Joseph II became Holy Roman Emperor; Leopold II also became Holy Roman Emperor following the death of Joseph II; and Maria Antonia, better known as Marie Antoinette, was queen of France (no. 40).

The death of her husband in 1765 dealt a heavy blow to Maria. She dressed only in black thereafter and ceded much of her power to her son, Joseph II.

Maria Theresa was a conservative ruler in both politics and religion. She strengthened her standing army and improved the economy through taxation. In the area of civil-rights reforms, she created the *Codex Theresianus* and outlawed witch burnings. At her death in 1780, Austria was in much better shape than when she took power 40 years earlier. She was one of the most powerful and influential women of the 18th century.

Maria Theresa's portrait first appeared on Austrian coins beginning in 1741. Because of the length of her reign, scores of coins of different types and denominations bear her portraits, from the small, silver kreuzers to the rare and valuable 10-ducat gold coin. Her image also appears on coins from the Austrian state of Burgau and on the coins of the Austrian Netherlands.

Maria Theresa wears a diadem and a veil on this large, silver taler. Though dated 1780, this is a modern restrike.

COLLECTING DIFFICULTY

Easy. Collectors have many options and opportunities when it comes to Maria Theresa's coins. Without a doubt, the best value is the Maria Theresa restrike—an old-school design made with modern technology on a large, silver planchet. They are dated 1780. These restrikes contain three-quarters of an ounce of silver, and can be purchased for close to their bullion value.

***Empress Maria Theresa of Austria*, by Martin van Meytens, circa 1759.**

No. 35

QUEEN ISABELLA II

Isabella's mother, Maria, was King Ferdinand's niece before she married him. Thus Isabella was simultaneously Maria's daughter and her cousin.

Queen Isabella II of Spain and her daughter, Isabella, **by Franz Xaver Winterhalter, circa 1852.**

Queen Isabella II ruled Spain from 1833 to 1868. She overcame the resistance of the men who fumed about a female ruler of Spain, she improved her country's railways, and she endured the revolts of the Spanish colonies in Puerto Rico and Cuba. She ended her life exiled in Paris in favor of the Glorious Revolution that eventually saw her son come to power.

Isabella was born in 1830 in Madrid to King Ferdinand VIII and Maria Cristina, his fourth wife, with whom he had hoped to produce a male heir. Unfortunately, Maria bore only daughters; thus, Ferdinand's younger brother, Carlos, was next in line for the throne. However, Ferdinand changed the law in 1830 (he was king, after all) to allow sons *or* daughters to succeed him. As a result, when Ferdinand died in 1833, his three-year-old daughter Isabella became queen, with her mother as regent. Carlos contested the succession immediately and went to war over the crown. Most of Spain remained loyal to Isabella as she successfully defended her title.

The effects of the contention between Isabella and Carlos can be seen in the Spanish coins of the time. The first coins of Isabella appeared in 1834, where she is shown as a young woman, designed that way so that her subjects might not notice that their country was actually being ruled by a four-year-old. As time progressed, the coins acted as snapshots of her life, and it is interesting to see her grow up over the 34 years in which she reigned. On the other side, Catalonia, a Spanish territory loyal to Carlos, issued coins known as "Pretender Coinage" in 1840, identifying Carlos (styled as Charles V) as king of Spain.

In 1868 Queen Isabella was forced into exile, and she spent the rest of her life in France.

Isabella appeared on Spanish coins from 1834 to 1868. The smallest coins that bear her portrait are the copper five centimos and the silver one real. The largest coins are the silver 20-real and 2-escudo coins. From 1864 to 1868, Isabella appears on a small number of coins from the Philippines.

Isabella II faces left on this 1858 Spanish 100-peseta gold coin.

COLLECTING DIFFICULTY

Easy. Isabellan coins are plentiful and often inexpensive. Even the gold coins from her reign are affordable. A type set of different denominations and designs would make an interesting collection.

No. 36

QUEEN GUINEVERE

Guinevere plays an important part in the book *The Mists of Avalon* by Marion Zimmer Bradley, who was married to the late Walter Breen, a well-known figure among U.S. coin enthusiasts.

Queen Guinevere was the wife of King Arthur in ancient lore. The numerous stories of Guinevere and her relationship with Arthur and Sir Lancelot vary widely based on the author and the time period. Thus, there is no clear and consistent image of Guinevere except that she was very beautiful.

In the earliest Welsh sources from the 11th century, Guinevere's name is spelled Gwenhwyfar. However, there is not one Queen Guinevere, but three. The first was unfaithful, shaming Arthur and setting the precedence for future depictions of Guinevere as an adulteress. In the 12th century, the second Guinevere descended from a noble Roman family. As time went on, the legend expanded. Soon Merlin can be seen warning King Arthur against marrying Guinevere because of her love for Lancelot, one of Arthur's knights. The third Guinevere, the daughter of King Leodegraunce of Cameoliard (sound familiar?), was a queen in her own right, with her own palace, and she brought the Round Table to Arthur as a dowry.

In early stories, Guinevere was abducted by King Melwas of Glastonbury. In later versions, Guinevere's abductors and rescuers change in name and place, creating a confusing tapestry of events.

Sir Lancelot, portrayed as one of her rescuers, was so smitten with Guinevere that he once fainted just at the sight of her. His love for her trumped his loyalty to his king, and the two engaged in an illicit romance. Arthur discovered the betrayal and was heartbroken. Ultimately, Arthur was killed in battle and Guinevere entered a convent and became a nun. Other versions of her demise were not so charitable.

Few coins bear a portrait of Guinevere. In 1996 the Isle of Man issued one-quarter–crown and one-crown coins bearing a depiction of Guinevere as part of their *Legend of King Arthur* series. The 1996 quarter crown exists in two bimetallic issues, one with platinum as one of the metals. The survey conducted for this book uncovered no other Guinevere coins, but an online search revealed one or two medals and even a casino token with her image.

The lovely Queen Guinevere holds a rose on this 1996 Isle of Man one-crown coin. She broke a king's heart.

COLLECTING DIFFICULTY

Easy, but the choices are limited to the Isle of Man coins.

***Queen Guinevere's Maying*, by John Collier.**

No. 37

LEDA AND THE SWAN

In 2007 the Flemish group Laïs used William Butler Yeats's poem, *Leda and the Swan*, as the lyrics for their song "Leda En de Zwaan (Agamemnon)."

Leda col Cigno, by Andrea del Sarto, circa 1490.

Leda was a female figure from Greek mythology whose interaction with the god Zeus produced four offspring, all of whom are perhaps better known today than their mother. The most famous of those children was Helen of Troy, the beautiful woman whose kidnapping provoked the Trojan War.

The myth of Leda and the Swan evolved over time, thus some details are hazy or intermingled. The gist of the story is that Leda's beauty attracted the attention of the god Zeus, who took the form of a swan and forced himself upon her. Leda gave birth to two eggs (or three, depending on the version of the story). The first egg produced Castor and Pollux (known as the *Dioskuri* in Greek, the *Gemini* in Latin, or the *Gemini Twins* in astrology). The second egg produced Clytemnestra and her sister Helen. Clytemnestra married Agamemnon, the king of Mycenae, and Helen married his brother, Menelaus.

By modern standards, the rape of Leda is disturbing, but such was the capricious nature of the gods in their dealings with humans. Consider the way in which the goddess Aphrodite offered Leda's daughter, Helen, as a bribe to Paris, her eventual abductor—conveniently leaving out the fact that Helen was already married.

Leda and the Swan was a popular theme in antiquity but exploded in art and sculpture during the Renaissance, where the depictions became more erotic and explicit. Famous artists such as Michelangelo, Leonardo da Vinci, Correggio, Francois Boucher, Salvador Dali, and others produced their own versions of the myth. An Internet search reveals hundreds of images of artistic variations on the Leda and the Swan theme, ranging from ancient to modern interpretations, from sculpture to cameos to paintings.

Currently, the only option for a Leda and the Swan coin is the colorized 2014 Cook Islands $20 piece which shows the famous painting by Peter Paul Rubens, whose work was based on a lost painting by Michelangelo. This is an oversized silver coin that has great visual appeal.

Many artists have attempted to portray the troubling legend of Leda mating with Zeus in the form of a swan. Peter Paul Ruben's version is one of the best.

COLLECTING DIFFICULTY

Easy, but limited to only one option. The 2014 Cook Islands $20 coin is readily available online but usually sells for $250 and up. Alternatives include a couple of different Leda and the Swan medals by Salvador Dalí.

No. 38

EDUCATION

James Smithson, the founder of the Smithsonian Institution in Washington, D.C., never visited America.

The female figure of Education represents teaching, knowledge, or the imparting of wisdom. Though no goddess of education exists in the ancient world, there are several goddesses who embodied wisdom. The list includes: Metis, the Greek Titan; Athena (see no. 27), the Greek goddess of wisdom, and Minerva (no. 27), her Roman equivalent; Lakshmi, the Hindu goddess; Seshat, the Egyptian goddess; and others. Some of these goddesses are depicted on coins, but for the purposes of this section, only coins with an anonymous figure of a teacher or an allegorical figure representing wisdom or education apply.

One such coin is the U.S. 1996 silver dollar commemorating the 150th anniversary of the Smithsonian Institution. The obverse of the coin features the "Castle," the original Smithsonian building. The reverse of the coin depicts a female sitting atop the Earth, holding a torch and a scroll that includes the words "Art, History, and Science." The phrase "For the Increase and Diffusion of Knowledge" (James Smithson's original mission statement) appears in the right field.

In 1979 Egypt struck a copper-nickel 10-piastre coin and a silver one-pound coin for either National Education Day or Teachers Day (sources vary). The reverse of the coin shows two teachers, back-to-back, instructing children. At least one of the tiny teachers is a female.

A proposed design for the 2015 and 2016 U.S. $100 platinum coins features "Wisdom" seated in a heavy chair holding a scale in her right hand (viewer's left), with a book of knowledge cradled in her left arm, and a sword of justice in her lap. Unlike Lady Justice, who is usually shown blindfolded, Wisdom has her eyes wide open. Whether this design will be accepted for use on coins remains to be seen.

In the medallic world, a new National Humanities Medal appeared in 2013 featuring a reclining Statue of Liberty, holding a lamp of knowledge in her left hand (viewer's right). This medal is given out each year by the U.S. president to deserving recipients in various disciplines.

In the paper-money world, the United States printed a series of *Educational* banknotes in 1896 depicting allegorical females presenting different subjects. For instance, the $1 note depicts History Instructing Youth.

A female personification of Education lights the world with knowledge on this 1996 U.S. silver dollar commemorating the 150th anniversary of the founding of the Smithsonian Institution.

COLLECTING DIFFICULTY

Easy. The Smithsonian dollar, the Egyptian 10-piastre coin, and the one-pound coins are readily accessible in the market. Prices vary, but they are all relatively inexpensive. For example, the Smithsonian silver dollar can be found for less than $50 in Proof.

Eugene Delaplanche's *L'education Maternelle* (Maternal Education), bronze with patina, 1873.

No. 39

EVE

One of the most hotly debated questions is whether or not Adam and Eve had navels. The great artist, Michelangelo, thought so—his depiction of Adam and Eve in the Sistine Chapel shows distinct belly buttons.

A serpent with a woman's head lurks in the Tree of Knowledge. Painting by Masolino da Panicale.

In the biblical story of creation, Eve was the first woman. The book of Genesis describes the loneliness of Adam, the first man, and how God fashioned a woman from a rib taken out of Adam's side as he slept. God created Eve to be a helper to Adam as he tended their home, the Garden of Eden.

Within the garden were various trees, including the Tree of Life and the Tree of the Knowledge of Good and Evil, both of which bore edible fruit. However, God expressly forbade the couple from eating of fruit of the Tree of the Knowledge of Good and Evil. The Devil, in the form of a serpent, convinced Eve that she would not be punished if she ate the forbidden fruit. She, in turn, convinced Adam that everything would be fine, so the couple ate the fruit; God found out about it and kicked them out of the Garden.

Eve bore at least two sons, Cain and Abel, and perhaps other children (the Bible references Cain's wife but does not explain from whence she came).

In the goddess lexicon, Eve is described as the "mother of all living," and she is similar to the women in alternative creation stories. In Hebrew, she is known as Hawwah. Eve has been likened to Ishtar of Babylonian legend, the Hindu goddess Kali, and her Aztec counterpart, Tlazalteol. Folkloric narratives show Eve in some interesting variations from the biblical story. For example, a Bulgarian version describes how Eve, originally created blind, receives her sight upon eating the forbidden fruit.

Eve is rarely shown on coins. In 2011 Palau issued a $2 coin as part of their *Biblical Stories* series that showed Eve taking a bite of one fruit and handing another to Adam. The trunk of the tree is entwined by a snake. A Vatican 50-lire coin of 1988 shows God breathing life into Eve as she arises from Adam's side. Also, Adam and Eve can be seen on a variety of silver art bars, Mardi Gras "doubloons," and medals.

Eve and Adam share a snack from the Tree of the Knowledge of Good and Evil on the obverse of this silver $2 coin made for sale to collectors. This was part of a *Biblical Stories* series of coins issued by Palau in 2011.

COLLECTING DIFFICULTY

Slightly difficult. Palau struck only 1,000 of the 2011 $2 coins, so they are definitely scarce and usually sell for substantial premiums over their catalog value. The Vatican coin is an inexpensive alternative, but it is decidedly more difficult to locate.

Marie Antoinette was the queen of France and reigned, along with her husband, King Louis XVI, from May 1774 until their executions in 1792. She was known for her beauty, poise, and grace, but also for her profligate spending. She was also the victim of smear campaigns throughout her reign, some of which had a basis in fact, others of which were baseless rumors designed to put her in a negative light.

Marie was born Archduchess Maria Antonia Josepha Johanna in November 1755, the daughter of the Austrian empress Maria Theresa (no. 34) and Emperor Francis I. She married the son of King Louis XV of France and left Austria forever in 1770. At first the French people embraced her, but through several missteps and scandalous rumors she soon fell out of favor. Despite France's considerable debt, the royal couple spent lavishly, eventually bankrupting the country. The people revolted and abolished the monarchy, leaving Marie and her husband at the mercy of the mobs. Both lost their heads to the guillotine in 1792.

Throughout numismatic history, many kings have honored their queens on coins, but such is not the case with Louis XVI. The average French person, looking at the coins in their hands, would never have known the queen existed. Marie does appear on numerous French medals, sometimes by herself, with her husband, or in celebration of their marriage. Marie also appears on several privately issued tokens and medals. Perhaps the most macabre is a 1795 halfpenny token by Peter Skidmore of England, which shows conjoined busts of Marie and her husband on the obverse. The reverse of the coins shows a guillotine with an empty basket waiting to catch her head. In 1997 Austria issued a 1,000-schilling gold coin with an obverse showing Marie Antoinette in all her finery. The reverse shows Marie at her Revolutionary trial, where she defended herself honorably against a foregone verdict of guilty (the image appears to have been taken from a contemporary print).

Marie Antoinette appears twice on this gold 1997 Austrian 1,000-schilling coin. On the obverse of the coin she is at her flamboyant best; on the reverse she is seen in a simple dress at her trial in 1793.

COLLECTING DIFFICULTY

Moderate. The Austrian 1,000-schilling coin is common but expensive because it contains half an ounce of gold. Medals and tokens with Marie Antoinette's image show up online in a variety of types and values.

No. 40

QUEEN MARIE ANTOINETTE

Only one of Marie Antoinette's children, Marie Thérèse, survived to adulthood. Her first son died of tuberculosis of the spine at age seven, her second son died in prison in 1795, and her second daughter died of tuberculosis at age 11 months.

***Marie Antoinette With the Rose*, by Vigée Le Brun (1783).**

No. 41

QUEEN HATSHEPSUT

As hard as they tried, the people who attempted to efface Hatshepsut's memory could not find every instance of her record. As more and more evidence is uncovered by archaeologists, the picture of Hatshepsut will become clearer, and her importance will be reinforced.

Stone statue of Hatshepsut.

Hatshepsut ruled Egypt from approximately 1479 to 1458 BC as regent for her stepson Thutmose III. She was the fifth ruler of the 18th dynasty, and she oversaw a nearly 22-year period of peace and prosperity. She styled herself more as a king than a queen and even adopted male clothing and the beard (albeit a false one) of the pharaohs. Unfortunately, much of what is known of Hatshepsut is speculation because, in later years, attempts were made to obliterate her name from Egyptian history.

Hatshepsut was the daughter of Thutmose I and Queen Ahmose. She had three, possibly four, step-brothers, all of whom were in line to be pharaoh, but they all predeceased their father except for Thutmose II. Upon their father's death, Hatshepsut and her half-brother, Thutmose II, married (such intermarriages were commonplace among the royal families) and bore a son, Thutmose III. After Thutmose II died, Hatshepsut became regent for her young son, and by the seventh year of her regency, perhaps even earlier, she was acknowledged as king of Egypt.

During her reign, Hatshepsut re-established trade routes that brought goods and wealth to Egypt. In one instance, she sent an expedition of ships to bring back frankincense trees. She built hundreds of buildings, monuments, and obelisks. The tallest obelisk of the ancient world, which still stands today, is attributed to Hatshepsut. Her colonnaded temple at Deir el-Bahri in the Valley of the Kings inspired later pharaohs to build monuments near hers.

Hatshepsut appears on several modern coins, including those of Egypt and Fiji. In 1994 Egypt issued a 5-pound silver coin depicting a limestone statuary head of Hatshepsut found in 1926 by the Metropolitan Museum of Art. It now lives in the Museum of Egyptian Antiquities in Cairo, Egypt. In 2012 Fiji issued multimedia, colorized silver $50 and $300 coins featuring a head of Hatshepsut wearing a striped nemes headdress. In the right field, a raised cartouche of Hatshepsut made of red jasper gemstone is glued to the coin.

Queen Hatshepsut appears in full pharaonic garb with her cartouche on a red gemstone in the right field. She wears a *nemes*—the same type of headdress worn by other pharaohs such as King Tutankhamen.

COLLECTING DIFFICULTY

Easy. The Fiji coin of Hatshepsut appears frequently online, usually at a price of $250 and up. The Egyptian coin rarely appears even though it has a large mintage and is less expensive.

No. 42

MEDUSA

Caravaggio's *Testa di Medusa* is on display at the Uffizi Gallery in Florence, Italy. The Sicilian flag includes the exact Medusa and triskelion symbol as seen on the Roman denarii of 49 BC.

Medusa was a hideous monster with venomous snakes for hair and a gaze that could turn any creature into stone. The rest of her story varies depending on the source. For instance, in the 1981 movie *Clash of the Titans*, Medusa is shown with glowing green eyes and a body in the shape of a serpent, replete with an ominous rattle at the end. Young Perseus (played by Harry Hamlin) avoided Medusa's glare with a reflective shield and was able to kill and behead her. He then flew on the back of the winged horse Pegasus, exposed Medusa's head to the Kraken, the giant sea-monster, and turned it into stone. He freed the lovely Andromeda and, presumably, the couple lived happily ever after. As is often the case, Hollywood jumbled up some of the characters in their story of Medusa, but there is enough variance in the ancient stories to forgive the foul.

In the Greek version, Medusa began life as a monstrous Gorgon. In the Roman version, she was a beautiful woman whom the goddess Minerva (no. 27) punished for having sex in her temple with the sea-god Neptune. Of the three Gorgons, only Medusa was mortal, which is why Perseus picked on her. From Medusa's beheaded body sprang her children by Neptune: the winged horse, Pegasus; and his brother, Chrysaor.

In 2009 the Cook Islands issued a colorized Medusa coin as part of their *Mystical Creatures* series. This coin features a bust of Medusa on the reverse and a bust of Queen Elizabeth II (no. 12) on the obverse. In 2010 Italy issued a 10-euro coin with the identical portrait of Medusa on the reverse (though not colorized) and a bust of Caravaggio, the Italian artist, on the obverse. Caravaggio's 1595 painting, *Testa di Medusa* (Head of Medusa), was the source of her portrait on both these coins. In 49 BC, Rome issued a silver denarius with the winged head of Medusa in the center of a triskelion. The reverse shows Jupiter holding a thunderbolt in his right hand (viewer's left) and an eagle in his right.

Don't look! Medusa's hideous head, with snakes for hair, could turn onlookers into stone.

COLLECTING DIFFICULTY

Easy. The Cook Islands Medusa dollar can be found in online auctions with ease. The Roman denarii featuring Medusa are all rare and valuable.

***Head of Medusa*, by Peter Paul Rubens, circa 1617–1618.**

No. 43

VICTORY

Victory is not to be confused with Christian angels, who also have wings on their backs (see no. 92), though it is possible that the depiction of angels may have been inspired by the ancient goddesses Nike and Victory.

Stone statue of Victory.

Victory (or Victoria) was the Roman incarnation of the goddess Nike (see no. 23). The Victory referred to here is the modern version, which may or may not adhere to the old Greek and Roman styles and may have a more secular, less religious meaning. In many cases, modern designers and engravers used Victory as an inspiration to elevate the artistry on the coins. For instance, Augustus Saint-Gaudens's design for the U.S. 1907 $20 gold piece featured a modified version of Victory, minus the wings and holding a torch and an olive branch instead of a palm frond. This popular design appeared on millions of $20 gold pieces from 1907 to 1933, then reappeared on the American Eagle gold bullion coins issued from 1986 to date.

The more classical, winged depictions of Victory can be seen on the 1990 1,000-lire coin of San Marino and the gold 50-peso piece issued by Mexico from 1921 to 1947. The 1979 500-lire coin of San Marino shows a woman driving a triga (a three-horse chariot), reminiscent of ancient Greek coins, with Nike holding the reins. However, here the word LIBERTAS identifies the woman as Liberty rather than Victory.

The statue atop the Brandenburg Gate in Berlin, Germany, is of Victory driving a quadriga (a four-horse chariot). Completed in 1791, the gate was then known as the Peace Gate, and the woman driving the quadriga was identified as Eirene, the goddess of Peace. In 1806 Napoleon of France defeated Prussia, marched through the gate, and took the statue back to Paris. In a game of military tag, Prussia drove Napoleon out of Germany in 1813 and sometime thereafter repatriated the statue. Karl Schinkel redesigned the statue by adding a Prussian eagle and an Iron Cross to the top of Victory's staff. This is a classic case of how goddesses have been interpreted and reinterpreted depending on their circumstances.

Winged Victory appears on the obverse of this large Mexican gold 50-peso coin of 1922. She holds a laurel wreath in her right hand.

COLLECTING DIFFICULTY

Easy. The San Marino coins mentioned above and the gold 50-peso coin of Mexico are all easy to obtain, thought the latter are expensive because they contain 1.2 ounces of gold.

No. 44

SAINT HELENA OF CONSTANTINOPLE

Images of Saint Helena often show her holding a cross, not unusual for a portrait of a saint. In her search for relics, she allegedly discovered the wooden cross on which Jesus was crucified. Purportedly, she found three crosses, and by testing them, she discovered that one possessed miraculous healing powers. Some of the relics she discovered are housed in the Basilica of the Holy Cross in Jerusalem in Rome, Italy.

Helena was an empress of the Roman Empire, the first wife of Constantius Chlorus (Constantius I), and the mother of Constantine the Great, the first Roman emperor to convert to Christianity. She is known alternatively as Saint Helena of Constantinople.

The exact date and place of Helena's birth are unknown but are believed to be around 250 AD in Drepanum (later renamed Helenopolis by her son), a city in Asia Minor. Helena's early life is largely unknown, but at some point she either married or cohabitated with Constantius. She bore his son, Constantine, around 272 AD. Constantius rose in power, and sometime before 289 AD, he divorced Helena. When her son rose to power, Helena was restored; Constantine then gave her the title "Augusta" (Empress). She spent much of the rest of her life travelling throughout the Middle East, establishing and improving churches, and searching for Christian relics.

Helena appears on numerous types of ancient coins, including bronze follisses and gold solidi. She usually appears on the obverse as a profile bust facing right. The reverses of her ancient coins are tied to allegorical figures representing Securitas (Security) and Pax Publica (Public Peace). Most of her coins were issued over a short period of time between 324 and 330 AD.

Romania produced a 500-lei gold coin in 2006 featuring Saint Helena and Constantine on the obverse. In 2010 the Cook Islands issued a colorized, rectangle-shaped $5 silver coin with a depiction of an iconic image of Saint Helena with a cross. A 2013 Bulgarian 100-leva gold coin shows Constantine and Saint Helena holding a Slavic cross between them.

Saint Helena as depicted on a Roman follis. Helena appears a second time as Securitas (Security), the robed figure on the reverse of the coin.

Saint Helena's name appears on this 1821 British East India Company half penny.

COLLECTING DIFFICULTY

Easy. Ancient coins bearing Helena's portrait are common and surprisingly inexpensive, ranging from $200 to $300 at the low end. Modern versions are more difficult to find because there are fewer different types, and they are not offered as frequently as the ancient coins.

***Helena of Constantinople,* by Cima da Conegliano, circa 1495.**

No. 45

FEMALE WORKER

Rosie the Riveter, one of the most famous icons of World War II, has never been honored on an American coin.

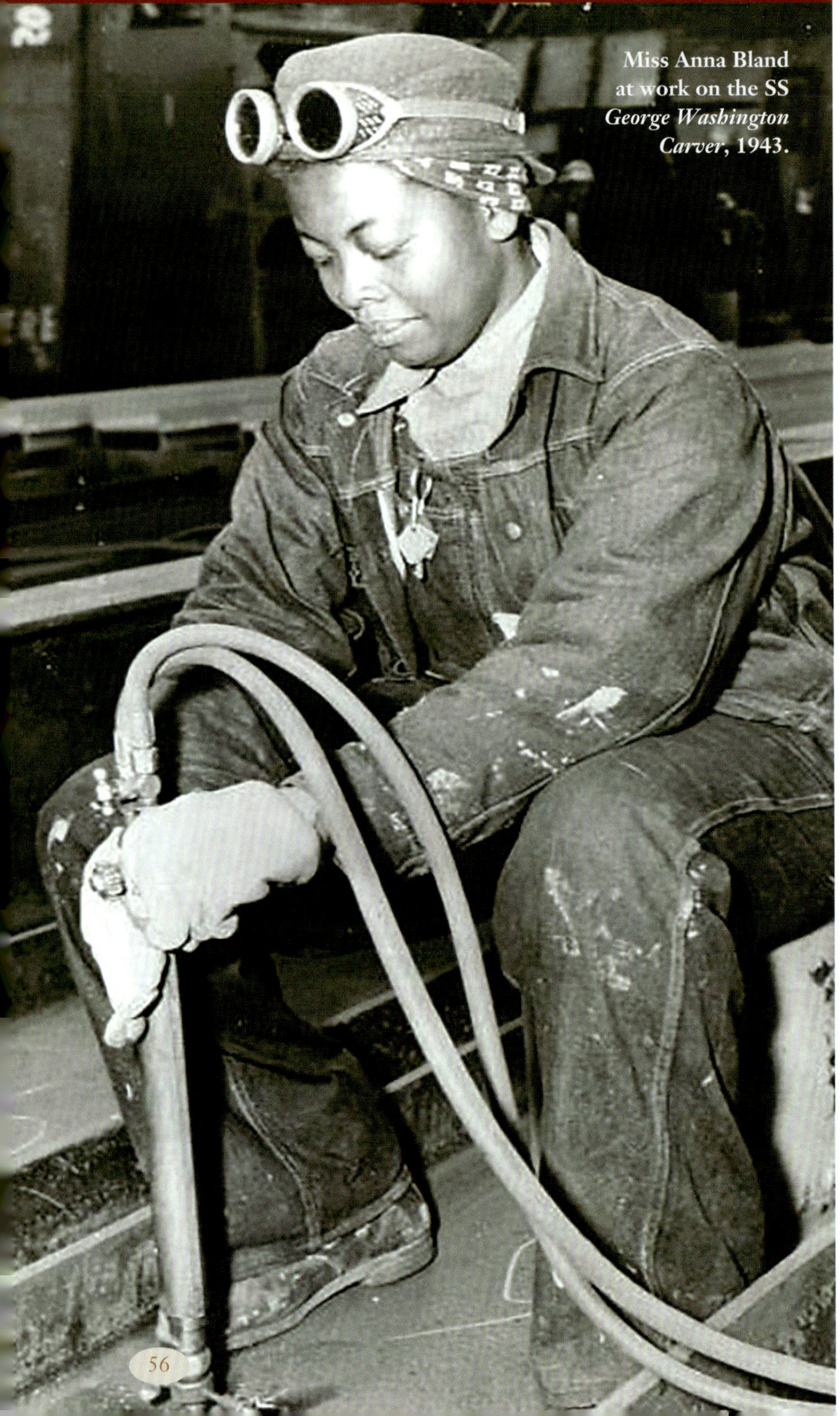

Miss Anna Bland at work on the SS *George Washington Carver*, 1943.

"Female worker" covers a lot of territory. For the purposes of this book, a female worker is any woman who is engaged in a money-making occupation, or in agriculture, or is simply a representation of the ideal worker. Since the beginning of time, women have worked to support and maintain their families, raise their children, support their husbands, and contribute to the success of society.

The concept of honoring workers seems to be a fairly recent one, especially where women are concerned. However, this is more a reflection of how society has changed in the past several decades. In America, World War II was the catalyst that brought many women into the workforce to support the men who had gone off to war (think Rosie the Riveter). For many American women, it was their first time in the workforce, the first time they earned money of their own, and their first taste of independence. Despite a few glass ceilings waiting to be broken, women nowadays can enter virtually any profession of their choice.

Female workers can be found on many coins. In France, the "Sower," a female sowing seeds by hand in a field, was a familiar figure on circulating coins from 1898 to 1914 and then again from 1960 until the present day. The Sower appears frequently on many several French commemorative coins, including the large 2009 50- and 100-euro coins honoring the 50th anniversary of the Court of Human Rights. Both China and Japan have honored female workers in the silk industry on commemorative coins. A 1995 China 5-yuan coin (KM-866) features a silk spinner at work. In 2013, as part of their *47 Prefectures Coin Program*, Japan issued 500- and 1,000-yen coins depicting women representative of workers in silk mills. In 1949 the new West German Republic struck a 50-pfennig coin with a woman planting a small oak tree, symbolizing the rebirth of the nation. 50 years later, in 1999, Bosnia-Herzogovina borrowed the same theme on an odd-denomination 14-euro coin that featured a woman planting "The Tree of Stability." For the Communist take on the female worker, try the 1979 20-mark coin (KM-75) honoring the 30th birthday of East Germany.

East Germany celebrated its 30th birthday as a country by honoring its male and female workers. The woman, wearing a scarf, occupies the secondary position.

COLLECTING DIFFICULTY

Easy. Most of the coins described here are common and inexpensive.

No. 46

JULIA GRANT

Julia was cross-eyed, a fact that is seldom noticeable in her photographs because she never faced the camera head-on. Julia and Mary Todd Lincoln disliked each other so much that the Grants declined, fortuitously as it turned out, an invitation to join the Lincolns at Ford's Theater the night that President Lincoln was assassinated.

Julia Grant was the wife of President Ulysses S. Grant, and as such the First Lady of the United States from 1869 to 1877. She was the first wife to serve eight years as First Lady since Elizabeth Monroe (who served from 1817 to 1825). During her time as First Lady, Julia refurbished the White House and made it the social center of Washington, D.C.

Julia was born Julia Boggs Dent in 1826 at the family's White Haven plantation in Grantwood Village, near St. Louis, Missouri. Her slave-holding family was well off and Julia attended a boarding school in St. Louis.

She met her future husband, Ulysses S. Grant, when he came to visit her brother at White Haven. Grant fell in love with Julia and her pleasant personality and eventually married her in 1848. Throughout the early years of their marriage and the Civil War, the Grants suffered long periods of separation and hardship. After Grant became president, Julia relished their time together and embraced her role as hostess at the White House.

Julia died in 1902, outliving her husband by 17 years. She spent her final years writing her memoirs, which were finally published in 1975. Julia's remains are interred along with her husband's in Grant's Tomb (now the General Grant National Monument) in Riverside Park in New York City, the same park where Eleanor Roosevelt's Monument is located.

In 2011 the United States honored Julia with a $10 gold First Spouse coin. The image on the obverse was taken from a portrait of Julia in the Library of Congress. The reverse of the coin shows a fictional rendering of Julia and a young Ulysses Grant riding horses at her family's plantation at White Haven. The Julia Grant First Spouse medal, struck in the same year in bronze, is nearly identical to the First Spouse coin minus several of the legends.

Julia Grant appeared on a U.S. 2011 First Spouse gold coin. The reverse of the coin shows Julia and her husband enjoying a ride together, one of their favorite pastimes.

This photograph of Julia Dent Grant was taken between 1869 and 1877.

COLLECTING DIFFICULTY

Easy, but the cost of the First Spouse coin can be high because it contains half an ounce of gold. As with all the First Spouse gold coins, the bronze medal is an attractive, less-expensive option.

No. 47

PERSEPHONE

In the Roman pantheon of gods, Persephone became Proserpina, and her mother, Demeter, became Ceres.

Proserpine, by Dante Gabriel Rosetti, circa 1874.

Persephone, in Greek mythology, was the daughter of Zeus and Demeter (no. 48). She was known both as the goddess of vegetation and the goddess of the underworld.

Persephone's beauty attracted the attention of the other gods, including Hermes, Apollo, and Hades. Demeter attempted to hide Persephone away, but Hades came up from the underworld in a crack in the earth and abducted her as she was gathering flowers with Artemis, Athena (no. 27), and the Oceanids. As she searched the world for her daughter, Demeter neglected the vegetation, and the people of Earth began to starve. Helios, the god of the sun, revealed to Demeter that Hades had taken Persephone to the underworld. Under pressure, Zeus forced Hades to return Persephone, on one condition: that she had not eaten anything in the underworld. Hermes went to retrieve her, but Hades tricked Persephone into eating some pomegranate seeds. Thus, Persephone was forced to return to the underworld every winter for a third of every year. When she returned to the upper world, vegetation flourished; when she returned to the underworld, the earth became barren, thus establishing the seasons.

In the Orphic religion, Persephone is the mother of Dionysius by Zeus, who seduced her in the guise of a serpent. To modern thinking, a father seducing his own daughter is disturbing, but incestuous relationships among the gods were not uncommon.

On ancient coins, Persephone is an oft-seen theme. Syracusian tetradrachms of 317 through 289 BC show Persephone as a young maiden. The title "Korae" (Koré or Cora) that appears on some coins is her name as a vegetation goddess, which translates to "maiden." Some coins of Sicily and Phrygia illustrate the Rape of Persephone with an image of Hades hauling her off in a quadriga (a chariot drawn by four horses).

The young, beautiful Persephone is featured on the obverse of this tetradrachm of Syracuse, Sicily. Her nickname, Korae, appears to the left of her head. The reverse of the coin shows the goddess Nike (see no. 23).

COLLECTING DIFFICULTY

Easy. Ancient Persephone coins are surprisingly common and offer a variety of different types and designs. Prices range from $200 to tens of thousands of dollars and everything in between.

Demeter was the Greek goddess of the harvest. She was the mother of Persephone (no. 47) in Greek mythology. They are so close that if one knows Persephone, then one knows Demeter, and vice versa; but their experiences in the legends differ dramatically. Nonetheless, in some instances, the two are indistinguishable from each other, as in Sicily, where they were both known as Damatres (Mothers). In Roman mythology, Demeter's counterpart was the goddess Ceres.

The fact that Persephone and Demeter rank next to each other at no. 47 and no. 48, respectively, in the list of the 100 Greatest Women on Coins is a remarkable coincidence. In the myths and legends, Demeter and Persephone were not only mother and daughter, but the two were also closely linked together as vegetation goddesses. They were also connected due to the sudden and horrific way in which they were ripped apart and the sad conclusion that they were never able to be together again as they wished.

Demeter appears on ancient and modern coins, but much more frequently on the former. In the ancient depictions, Demeter usually wears a crown of grains, or she may appear with symbols of agriculture such as ears of wheat or corn (see the illustration here of a Roman silver denarius from around 64 BC). The "crown of grains" theme appears on some French silver coins beginning in 1848, where Liberty's bust is known as a "Ceres" head. In 1994 the Marshall Islands issued $10 brass coins as part of their *Wonders of the Solar System* series. On the coin representing the Earth, Demeter is shown as a symbolic mother, seated with two children. In 1995 Andorra produced a 10-diner coin to promote the Food and Agricultural Organization of the United Nations with, appropriately, an image of Demeter holding a bunch of wheat stalks and ears in her arms. Greece issued a 10-drachma coin in 1930 with a classical Greek head of Demeter facing left; her name appears in Greek letters along the right border.

The goddess Demeter appears on the obverse of this silver denarius of ancient Rome. Dated to 64 BC, the coin shows Demeter's profile facing right. An ear of wheat and a barleycorn flank her portrait.

COLLECTING DIFFICULTY

Easy. Many collectors are surprised to learn how common and inexpensive ancient coins can be. For instance, a nearly Mint State Demeter coin sometimes sells for $1,000 or less. Imagine a silver coin that is over 2,000 years old that is nearly as nice as the day it was made—they exist and they are within reach.

No. 48

DEMETER

Demeter, as an earth mother, has been likened to the Greek goddess Gaia, but Demeter is actually Gaia's granddaughter. Demeter was born of the Titans Cronus and Rhea, both of whom were Gaia's children.

***Ceres and Pan*, by Peter Paul Rubens and Frans Snyders, circa 1615.**

No. 49

EMPRESS JULIA DOMNA

Julia wore a distinctive hairstyle of parallel ridges that extended backwards from her face and braids tied together at the back of her head.

Bust of Julia Domna, probably wearing a wig.

Julia Domna was empress of the Roman Empire during the reign of her husband, Lucius Septimius Severus (193 to 198 AD). She was one of the most powerful women of her time, and she wielded considerable influence during and following her husband's death, up until her suicide in 217 AD. She was deeply interested in philosophy, prompting the nickname Julia the Wise.

Julia was born in the Syrian city of Emesa around 170 AD. She came from an extremely wealthy family, and she caught the attention of Septimius Severus, then a Roman senator who had been born in North Africa. At the time of their marriage in 187, Septimius was already at least 25 years older than Julia. The couple had two sons, Lucius Septimius Bassianus (Caracalla) and Publius Septimius Geta (Geta). Julia's marriage to Septimius was a good one, and she accompanied him on several of his military campaigns. Following Septimius's death in 198, their two sons became co-emperors under Julia's guidance. However, tragedy soon struck when Roman centurions murdered Geta in her arms, allegedly at the instigation of Caracalla. After six years of rule, Caracalla himself was assassinated. Stricken with grief, alone in the world, and suffering from a tumor in her breast, Julia starved herself to death in 217.

Julia Domna appears on numerous silver denarii and gold aurei. On certain coins, she is called Matri Castrorum (Mother of the Camp) in recognition of her attendance during the military campaigns of her husband and her son Caracalla. On a Roman denarius of approximately 202 AD, Julia is shown on the reverse flanked by her sons Geta and Caracalla; Severus appears on the obverse. On later coins she is shown on the obverse with her two sons on the reverse. On other coins, Julia is titled Mother of the Emperors, Mother of the Senate, and Mother of her Country—these coins were issued after her husband died and while she guided imperial Rome during Caracalla's absences. After Caracalla's ascension to sole power, he issued denarii with conjoined busts of himself and his mother on the reverse.

Julia Domna on both the obverse and reverse of a gold aureus of approximately 211 AD. The reverse legend reads: "Mother of the Emperors, Mother of the Senate, and Mother of her Country."

COLLECTING DIFFICULTY

Easy to moderately difficult. Roman denarii featuring Julia alone are fairly common and inexpensive. Those picturing her with either of her two sons are more expensive, often running into four figures. Gold aurei can be quite expensive, especially in nice condition.

No. 50

QUEEN BOUDICA

The Welsh name for Boudica was "Buddug." Boudica translates to Victoria in English, and, during Queen Victoria's reign, myth-builders attempted to tie the two together.

Boudica was queen of the Iceni, a Celtic tribe from the region surrounding modern-day Norwich, on the east side of England. She is famous for her failed rebellion against the Romans in 60 or 61 AD. Queen Boudica was described as a tall woman with waist-length, tawny hair, a terrifying appearance, a fierce gaze, and a harsh voice. Both virtuous and barbaric, Boudica remains one of the most compelling women in British history.

What we know of Boudica comes primarily from Tacitus and Lucius Cassius Dio, both of whom were Roman historians. Because no British histories exist to counter the Roman narratives, the story of Queen Boudica is somewhat lopsided. Adding to the confusion are numerous legends and myths that arose over the past several hundred years. Even her name is in dispute, though scholars have come to some agreement that "Boudica" was the proper, contemporary usage, and that "Boudicca" and "Boudicea" are more modern versions.

Boudica might have been just a minor footnote in history except that her husband named his two daughters and the Roman emperor as co-heirs to his kingdom. Upon the king's death, the Romans ignored his will, annexed the kingdom, flogged Boudica, and raped her daughters. Justifiably provoked to revolt, Boudica rallied Britons to her side and plundered and destroyed the cities of Camulodunum (modern-day Colchester), Londinum (modern-day London), and Verulamian (modern-day Saint Albans). According to Tacitus, Boudica and her army slaughtered almost 80,000 Romans. Eventually Boudica met defeat at the hands of a Roman force led by Gaius Suetonius Paulinus, in 60 or 61 AD Depending on the source, the vanquished Boudica either committed suicide or died of an illness.

Boudica is believed to appear on Celtic coins of the Iceni issued during the first century BC, but the image is so crude that a positive attribution cannot be made. Boudica again appears on a 2004 East Caribbean States coin of $2 face value. She is shown riding a biga (a chariot drawn by two horses), inspiring her warriors to battle.

The fierce warrior-queen Boudica is shown leading her troops in battle on the reverse of this 2004 East Caribbean States coin of $2 face value.

COLLECTING DIFFICULTY

Moderate, with a twist. Boudica coins, even the ancient ones, are relatively inexpensive, but they are difficult to locate outside of auctions of ancient coins.

Statue of Queen Boudica in London.

No. 51

SAINT HILDEGARD OF BINGEN

A bronze sculpture of Hildegard von Bingen, created in 1998 by Karlheinz Oswald, stands in front of the Eibingen Abbey. Hildegard has never been canonized by the Catholic Church as an official saint, though she is referred to as such.

Print of Hildegard von Bingen.

Hildegard of Bingen was a Roman Catholic nun who was a prolific writer, composer, preacher, herbalist, and mystic. Had she lived several hundred years later, she would have been described as a "Renaissance" woman. Her books and letters are among the most important medieval manuscripts to have survived.

Hildegard was born in 1098 in Bickelheim, Germany, the youngest of 10 children born to a knight and a noble woman. She was educated at a local monastery and became a Benedictine nun around her 18th birthday. From a young age Hildegard had spiritual visions, which she kept largely to herself. At age 42, she had a life-changing spiritual vision that she claimed gave her insight into God's Word. She recorded many of her fantastical visions as illuminations in her book, *Scivias* (Know the Ways). In 1151, she started a new monastery at Rupertsburg, placing it under the leadership of the Archbishop of Mainz and the protection of the emperor. She began travelling and preaching throughout Germany and even into Switzerland and France, promoting justice and morality and railing against corruption and error in the Catholic Church. She corresponded with earthly and spiritual leaders, she composed liturgical songs, and she wrote books on the causes and cures of human diseases and the medicinal qualities of plants and animals. She died in 1179 at the age of 81.

In 1998 West Germany issued a 10-mark silver coin celebrating the 900th anniversary of Saint Hildegard's birth. The obverse of the coin depicts Hildegard transcribing a vision she is receiving from the hand of God. A banner bears the words *LIBER SCIVIAS DOMINI* (Latin for "Know the Ways of the Lord"). In 2008 a private firm made a special geo-cache medal bearing the image of Hildegard on the obverse; the reverse features a rendering of one of Hildegard's book illuminations described as "Cultivating the Cosmic Tree." Numerous Catholic medals and pendants bear her image.

This 1988 West German 10-mark coin shows Saint Hildegard receiving one of her visions from God.

COLLECTING DIFFICULTY

Easy. The 1998 Germany 10-mark coin is readily available in Uncirculated and Proof versions at affordable prices. The geo-cache medal is an interesting representation of Hildegard, but it is surprisingly difficult to locate.

No. 52

YELLOW ROSE

It is unclear when the nose art was first added to the Yellow Rose, but she has undergone at least one revision. An earlier, pre-1986 version of Yellow Rose was nude, prompting complaints from the public that led to the addition of her skimpy vest and skirt.

Yellow Rose was an example of "nose art" used primarily in World War II to individualize planes. Nose art was a form of expression used by fighter pilots and bomber crews, and it was one of the few breaks from military regimentation and uniformity. The simplest nose-art designs consist of names (the Enola Gay, the plane that dropped the atomic bombs on Hiroshima and Nagasaki, Japan, features perhaps the most famous example), nicknames, and slogans. More elaborate nose art included cartoons, devils, orchids, and lots of women, particularly pinup girls.

The Yellow Rose was a B-25 "Mitchell" Bomber built in 1943 and delivered on April 26, 1944. This model was nicknamed after General William "Billy" Mitchell, the World War I Army general who is considered the "Father of the United States Air Force." 16 B-25s participated in "Dolittle's Raid" on April 18, 1942, the first air raid of Japan.

The Yellow Rose never saw action overseas during World War II but was assigned to units in South Carolina, Connecticut, and Massachusetts before being put into storage in Texas in 1946. Beginning in 1949, the Yellow Rose served as a ground instructional airframe for seven years before being restored to flying status in 1956 and used to train pilots. After a complete restoration, the plane was donated in 1981 to the Commemorative Air Force of San Marcos, Texas. Today it travels around the country to various air shows where visitors can climb aboard and travel back in time to World War II. The plane is one of about 30 B-25s that are still airworthy today.

In 2012 the island nation of Niue issued a three-coin set commemorating World War II nose art. Included in the set are colorized silver $2 coins featuring the *Yellow Rose*, *Briefing Time*, and the *Memphis Belle*. The coins come in a metal box with a descriptive mini-brochure.

Yellow Rose, as she appears on the nose of a fully restored World War II bomber that is still flying today. In the modern version, Yellow Rose is dressed more modestly than she was in the original.

COLLECTING DIFFICULTY

Easy, with a caveat. Collectors rarely break up the three-coin sets issued by Niue; to obtain this single coin, the only option is to purchase the entire set. On the positive side, the set contains three women on coins, of which Yellow Rose is the only one in the 100 Greatest.

Nose art of the *Memphis Belle*.

No. 53

TERESA DE FRANCISCI

Teresa and her husband both died on October 20. He died in 1964 and she died 26 years later in 1990.

Teresa de Francisci was the wife of Anthony de Francisci, the artist/sculptor who created the design for the U.S. Peace dollar, first issued in 1921. Her face—or more properly, her husband's version of her face—has appeared on more than 180 million coins.

Teresa was born Mary Teresa Cafarelli in a town south of Naples, Italy, in 1898. She immigrated with her family to the United States when she was four years old and moved to Clinton, Massachusetts, where she graduated from high school. Two years later, in 1920, she married Anthony de Francisci, an up-and-coming sculptor who, like Teresa, was of Italian descent. In late 1921, Anthony entered a design competition for a new Peace dollar. Time was of the essence, as Anthony and the seven other artists invited to participate in the competition had less than three weeks to prepare their designs and models in order to have the coins ready by the end-of-the-year deadline. Because of the time crunch, Teresa served as the model for the bust of Liberty that appears on the front of the coin.

There is no doubt that Teresa was the model for the Peace dollar. Contemporary profile portraits of her are an almost exact match. Teresa described seeing "herself" on the Peace dollar as the fulfillment of a childhood dream. A photograph from 1922 shows Anthony and Teresa standing together as he works on a round plaster with his gaze directly on her. However, Anthony admitted that the portrait was not an exact photographic image of Teresa, but one that symbolized American ideals. He also admitted that the whole face had been elongated.

De Francisci's Peace dollars dated 1921 appeared in the earliest days of 1922. The high-relief details of the first version slowed production, necessitating a reduction in the relief for the 1922-dated issues. The Mints at Philadelphia, Denver, and San Francisco all contributed to Peace dollar production from 1921 to 1928 and from 1934 to 1935.

A rare photo of Teresa de Francisci.

This matte Proof version of a 1922 Peace dollar is among the most perfect examples of Anthony de Francisci's work. Miss Liberty, as modeled by Teresa de Francisci, appears in high-relief detail.

COLLECTING DIFFICULTY

Easy. Peace dollars are readily available in both circulated conditions and Mint State. Common, circulated dates can be purchased for less than $20, and Mint State versions can be found for $30 and up.

In 2008 the tiny principality of Andorra issued a rectangular 10-diner coin commemorating Pierre-Auguste Renoir as part of their *Great Painters of the World* series. The obverse presents a partially colorized version of his *Two Young Girls at the Piano*, with the two girls shown in glittering silver. The reverse of the coin shows a portrait of Renoir beneath a palette bearing a colorized image of the *Bust Portrait of Jeanne Samary*.

Two Young Girls at the Piano was painted by Pierre-Auguste Renoir in 1892, shortly after his 50th birthday. This was the first painting Renoir ever sold to the French government, signaling the great respect he had earned as a painter. Henry Roujon, the French director of fine arts, purchased the painting for 4,000 francs, one of the highest prices Renoir had ever received for a painting up to that time. When he painted *Two Young Girls*, Renoir was already suffering from rheumatoid arthritis, which would afflict him and limit his ability to paint for the rest of his life.

Renoir painted the *Bust Portrait of Jeanne Samary* in 1877. Jeanne Samary was only 20 years old at the time, but she was already a famous actress. She modeled for Renoir on several occasions.

Renoir lived from 1841 to 1919 and was one of the leading Impressionist painters. At 15 he apprenticed to a porcelain factory, where he painted plates and vases. After hours, he attended art classes, and from 1860 to 1864 he spent time in the Louvre museum copying paintings. He entered numerous paintings in the Paris Salon competitions, hoping to find recognition there. After several disappointing showings, he exhibited in 1874 at an independent show which was mocked by critics as the "Exhibition of the Impressionists," a name that eventually took on more positive meanings. In 1879 Renoir finally achieved success in the Salon with *Mme. Charpentier and Her Children*. He painted on commission, usually portraits, but he also painted numerous nudes, cityscapes, landscapes, and fanciful compositions.

Renoir died in 1919 after having painted several thousand works.

Renoir and his paintings, *Girls at the Piano* and *Bust Portrait of Jeanne Samary*, are immortalized on this Andorran 10-diner coin of 2008.

COLLECTING DIFFICULTY

Easy. The Andorran 10-diner coin shows up on the secondary market quite frequently, and there are always three or four available online at any given time. The pricing is highly variable, so be sure to search for the least expensive example.

No. 54

TWO YOUNG GIRLS AT THE PIANO, BY RENOIR

Andorrans have the highest life expectancy in the world. In 1990 Sotheby's sold Renoir's *Au Moulin de la Galette* for $78.1 million, the second-highest price ever paid for a painting at the time.

Full painting of *Two Young Girls at the Piano* by Renoir.

No. 55

QUEEN CLEOPATRA I SYRA

Following her marriage to Ptolemy V, Cleopatra received the titles *Thea Epiphanes* and *Thea Eucharistos*, meaning "manifest goddess" and "beneficent goddess." Following Ptolemy V's death, she became "Cleopatra the mother, the manifest goddess." Often her name appeared before that of her husband or son, indicating the high regard in which she was held.

Marble bust, possibly of Cleopatra I Syra, 2nd century BC.

Cleopatra I Syra (also known as the Syrian) was born in or around the year 204 BC as the first of numerous Cleopatras from Egypt. She was no relation to the Cleopatras of earlier times (for instance, Alexander the Great had a sister named Cleopatra). The lineage of the Egyptian Cleopatras is confusing because the numbering system isn't consistent, but this Cleopatra was the first of the Egyptian queens, and her descendant Cleopatra VII (no. 4 among the 100 Greatest Women on Coins) was the last.

Cleopatra I was one of at least three children of Antiochus III (the Great), king of the Seleucid Empire, and his wife, Queen Laodice III. The Seleucid Empire had resulted from the carving up of Alexander the Great's empire following his death, and it covered a wide swath across the central portion of Asia. The Ptolemaic empire was also a former part of Alexander's empire and included much of northeast Africa, of which Egypt was a part. Conflict between the Seleucid and Ptolemaic empires ensued, and Antiochus offered his daughter, Cleopatra, in marriage to Ptolemy V of Egypt in an attempt to smooth over the difficulties. Their wedding took place in 193 BC in Raphia, a neutral city near the border of the two great empires. Cleopatra was approximately 11 years old and Ptolemy around 17 when they married.

The couple had three children: Cleopatra II, Ptolemy VI Philometer (Mother-Loving), and Ptolemy VIII Physcon (Pot-Bellied). When Cleopatra I's husband died in 180 BC, she became co-ruler with her son, Ptolemy VI, since he was a young boy at the time. After an uneventful reign, Cleopatra I died in 176 BC.

Cleopatra I appears on several Ptolemaic coins. On bronze coins, her head faces right and she appears as a deified Isis. Gold octodrachms struck in the name of Arsinoe II are often ascribed to Cleopatra I, but these were issued over such a long period of time that it seems questionable that the portrait is that of Cleopatra.

Though struck in the name of Arsinoe II, the diademed head on this Ptolemaic octodrachm is often attributed to Cleopatra I.

COLLECTING DIFFICULTY

Moderate. Bronze coins showing Cleopatra as Isis are fairly common and inexpensive, often available for less than $200. Gold octodrachms, on the other hand, are quite expensive and can run upwards of $7,500.

No. 56

QUEEN CLEOPATRA SELENE II

Cleopatra means "glory to the father." It was a popular name in ancient times but is less common today. According to thinkbabynames.com, Cleopatra ranked 2,655th in popularity out of 4,276 names in the 2000 U.S. census.

Cleopatra Selene II (hereafter Selene) was the daughter of the Roman emperor Mark Antony and Cleopatra VII (no. 4 among the 100 Greatest Women on Coins). She and her twin brother, Alexander Helios, were born in 40 BC, approximately 100 years after her namesake, Cleopatra Selene I. In Greek mythology, Selene was the goddess of the moon, and Helios was the god of the sun, so it is not surprising that Antony and Cleopatra gave their children celestial names of great significance.

Following Cleopatra VII's death in 30 BC, the young Selene became a ward of the Roman emperor Octavian, who brought her to Rome and paraded her in his triumphal procession along with a statue of her mother (who had committed suicide to avoid this ignominy). Selene, Alexander, and their brother Ptolemy Philadelphus were raised by Octavia, Antony's fourth wife, whom he had abandoned for Cleopatra VII—one can only imagine how grating the presence of his children by another woman must have been to Octavia.

Little is known of Selene's later life except that around 20 BC she married Juba II of Numidia, himself a prize captured by Julius Caesar in his African campaigns. At some point, the couple moved to Mauretania (corresponding with modern-day Morocco) and had a son, Ptolemy. The exact date of Selene's death is unknown, but could have been as early as 5 AD and as late as 17 AD. She was the last of the royal queens of Egypt, and her son, Ptolemy, was the last of her line.

Selene appears on silver denarii of Mauretania, opposite her husband, King Juba. Their portraits are simple and nondescript, yielding no clue as to their true appearance. Cleopatra is mentioned on several other Juban denarii, where her name might appear with a Nile crocodile, a moon and star, or a headdress of Isis and a lyre.

Simple depictions of Cleopatra Selene II and her husband, King Juba II of Mauretania, appear on this silver denarius.

COLLECTING DIFFICULTY

Easy. Coins with her portrait are more difficult to locate than coins with her name, thus it depends on how "pure" a collector wishes to be. The coins featuring crocodiles are among the most curious of ancient denarii, and since Selene's face is indistinct on coins where her portrait appears, they are a tempting alternative.

This 2nd century BC bust, thought by some to depict Cleopatra Selene II, is housed in the Louvre.

No. 57

FEMALE SLAVE

Not only did the U.S. Constitution fail to abolish slavery, it legalized the importation of slaves until 1808 under the Slave Trade Clause (Article 1, Section 9, Clause 1). After 1808 slavery continued to be legal in America until the 13th Amendment in 1865. Brazil was the last country in the Americas to abolish slavery.

Portrait of a female slave, by Annibale Carraci.

Slavery has been a stain on human history from ancient times up until today, even at the time of publication. Slavery is about domination, disregard for human dignity, and the exploitation of one person to the benefit of another. The plight of female slaves is especially egregious because of the sexual component that often accompanies. While male slaves were used primarily for manual labor, female slaves were and are sometimes used for sexual gratification. The story of Thomas Jefferson and Sally Hemmings is but one example of an illicit relationship between a master and a slave.

Slavery in the American colonies was a logical extension of the legal slavery that existed throughout the British Empire. The U.S. Constitution did not outlaw slavery but addressed it in a twisted fashion by counting slaves as three-fifths of a person for purposes of representation in Congress, though no slaves were allowed to vote. While other countries began to outlaw slavery (Great Britain banned the slave trade in 1807, for example, and made all slavery illegal in 1833), the matter continued to be a contentious issue in the United States until it was resolved by the Civil War.

In 1998 Brazil issued three 100-cruzado coins celebrating the 100th anniversary of the abolition of slavery in that country. One of the coins features a three-quarters profile of an anonymous female slave on the front; another features a male slave; and the third, a child slave. All three coins bear the greeting "Axé," which translates loosely to "Peace." In 1838 a private manufacturer in America struck copper anti-slavery tokens in the size of a one-cent piece. The obverse depicted a female slave in chains, kneeling and pleading for her freedom, "Am I Not a Woman and a Sister?" This theme and slogan originated in England in 1787 and became a popular abolitionist image for decades thereafter. A British token struck by Thomas Halliday in 1834 bore the same iconic message in a slightly modified and expanded version.

A female slave appears on the front of this Brazilian 100-cruzado coin, issued in 1988 to commemorate the 100th anniversary of the abolition of slavery in that country.

COLLECTING DIFFICULTY

Easy. The Brazilian 100-cruzado coin is common, inexpensive, and easy to obtain. Anti-slavery tokens are scarce, but not rare, and the prices range from reasonable to expensive depending on the type and condition. For example, low-grade British anti-slavery tokens of the late 1700s can be obtained for less than $100, while more elaborate medals of the 1800s can cost upwards of $500.

No. 58
GERMANIA

The author's favorite portrayal of Germania is in an 1828 painting by Johann Friedrich Overbeck, titled *Italia und Germania.* Germania, on the right, sits holding hands with Italia, their heads nearly touching, clearly symbolizing the close relationship between their two countries.

Germania is the female personification of Germany. Like Miss Liberty of the United States, she is presented on a wide variety of media in equally diverse forms. For instance, in paintings, she might be displayed as soft and feminine or as firm, resolute, and warlike (think Valkyrie). Sometimes she is shown holding a flag, a sword, or a shield. Often the composition includes a black imperial eagle.

Perhaps the most famous expression of Germania in sculpture is in the *Niederwalddenkmal*, a monument on the northern banks of the Rhein River near Rudesheim am Rhein, Germany. Surrounded by woods and vineyards atop a rising hill, the 34-foot-tall Germania stands atop a massive stone monument and commands the countryside. She stands in front of a seat fashioned with fierce eagles on either side. Her left hand holds aloft the imperial German crown, and her right hand holds a massive sword. Her breastplate is emblazoned with an imperial eagle. Her long hair trails behind.

Germania appears on numerous German coins, medals, and pattern issues. On coins of Frankfurt, such as the thalers and double thalers of 1859 to 1866, Germania is shown as a young lady facing right, her hair up in a bun with a wreath of oak leaves. On a Frankfurt shooting thaler of 1862, Germania stands steadying a large shield bearing a double-headed eagle, her right arm outstretched with a victor's wreath in her hand. German pattern coins show Germania in a variety of different poses. For instance, she appears on a 1908 25-pfennig pattern wearing an armored breastplate and a crown atop her head. In the 1920s the noted medalist Karl Goetz returned to softer portrayals of Germania as a young *mädchen*. In 1999 Palau issued a $5 coin as part of their *International Coins* series. On the reverse, Germania is shown next to the colonial arms of Cameroon, a German colony from 1884 to the end of World War I.

A young, feminine Germania graces a double thaler of Frankfurt. The oak leaves in her hair represent heroism.

COLLECTING DIFFICULTY

Easy. Frankfurt thalers are plentiful, though the double thalers are more scarce and valuable. In general, German pattern coins are very rare, but the Goetz Germania patterns are a delightful exception.

Statue of Germania over the Rhine.

No. 59

ANNE OF GREEN GABLES

The real Green Gables farm in Cavendish, Prince Edwards Island, was the inspiration for L.M. Montgomery's book. It is a popular tourist destination, especially for Japanese couples who travel there to get married.

Lealand Gustavson painted this movie-promotion illustration in 1934.

Anne of Green Gables was a book written in 1908 by L.M. (Lucy Maud) Montgomery, of which more than 50 million copies had been sold by its centennial in 2008. Much of the allure of *Anne of Green Gables* can be attributed to Montgomery's exceptional writing style and the heroine's feisty character and indomitable spirit. The main character of the book is an 11-year-old orphan named Anne Shirley, who is sent to the Cuthberts, an elderly brother and sister who own a farm—Green Gables—in Prince Edwards Island, Canada. Anne, who lost both her parents at a young age, had been in and out of families. Just prior to going to the Cuthberts, she spent four months in an orphan asylum. Despite suffering from years of neglect, poverty, and a lack of love, Anne maintained an optimistic spirit in which she saw the good in everything, and she developed a hyperactive imagination to turn the ordinary into the extraordinary. Anne's arrival at Green Gables surprises the Cuthberts, who had sent for a boy to help them on the farm, but Anne's pitiful situation and lovable personality quickly wins them over. The remainder of the story presents Anne's adventures and misadventures while at Green Gables. The book is alternately sad and hilarious, and usually has a moral undercurrent. The end of the book, without giving anything away, is bittersweet, with Anne, as a young adult, facing the future with her eternally optimistic attitude.

Montgomery wrote seven sequels to Anne of Green Gables, as well as other novels and essays, and hundreds of poems and short stories.

In 2008 Penguin Books commissioned author Budge Wilson to write *Before Green Gables*, a story of Anne's life before she joined the Cuthberts.

To commemorate the 100th anniversary of the *Anne of Green Gables* book, Canada issued an oversized 25-cent coin with a colorized portrait of Anne with her red pigtails and white frock, holding a bouquet of yellow flowers.

In 2008 Canada commemorated the 100th anniversary of the book *Anne of Green Gables* with this oversized 25-cent piece.

COLLECTING DIFFICULTY

Easy. The Canadian 2008 "Anne of Green Gables" quarter is inexpensive and easy to obtain.

No. 60

QUEEN BEATRIX

Unlike many monarchies, where kings and queens ruled until their death, the queens of the Netherlands abdicated to allow for an orderly succession. Both Beatrix and her mother, Juliana, abdicated on Queen's Day. When Willem-Alexander became king, the holiday became known as King's Day.

Beatrix Wilhelmina Armgard was queen of the Netherlands from 1980 until 2013, when she abdicated in favor of her son, Prince Willem-Alexander. She was the third in a line of queens who ruled the Netherlands for 128 consecutive years, beginning with Emma, who ruled as regent from 1890 to 1898; Wilhelmina, who ruled from 1898 until 1948; and Juliana (see no. 62), who reigned from 1948 until 1980.

Beatrix was born in January 1938, the daughter of Queen Juliana of the Netherlands and her husband, Prince Bernhard of Lippe-Biesterfeld (a line of the German House of Lippe). During World War II Juliana and her two daughters evacuated to Canada, where they stayed until May 1945, when they returned to the Netherlands. In 1961 Beatrix earned a law degree and, in 1966, she married Claus von Amsberg of Germany. The couple had three children. She became queen of the Netherlands in April 1980, following her mother's abdication.

The first appearance of Beatrix on a circulating coin was in 1980, when the Netherlands struck special coins commemorating her investiture. In that year Beatrix and her mother, Juliana, appear together. The Netherlands has a history, at least in modern times, of innovative coin designs, and there are numerous commemorative coins that present Beatrix in a variety of creative ways. For instance, the 1988 50-gulden coin struck to commemorate the 300th anniversary of the beginning of the reign of William and Mary of England presents Beatrix's head in an unusual cross-hatch pattern. Two years later, the Netherlands struck a 50-gulden coin to celebrate 100 years of Dutch queens. On this coin, Beatrix appears as a head made of a series of lines evocative of a fingerprint; on the reverse, the four queens are shown as rocks. A Netherlands 2003 5-euro piece fashioned the heads of Beatrix and Vincent Van Gogh out of words and letters.

Queen Beatrix appears with Vincent Van Gogh on this special Dutch 5-euro coin commemorating the 150th anniversary of the artist's birth.

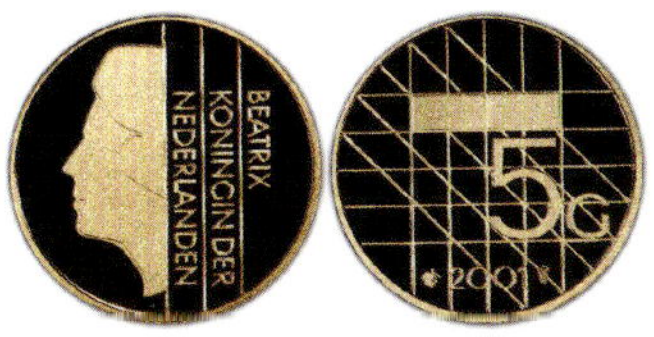

The Netherlands has a history of innovative coin designs, and this 2001 gold 5-gulden piece is no exception.

COLLECTING DIFFICULTY

Easy. The length of her reign generated decades of coins with Beatrix's image, many of which are common and inexpensive. The wide variety of types and the fascinating array of designs are a fertile field for a Beatrix-themed collection.

Queen Beatrix at her last official meeting with the prime minister before her abdication.

No. 61

HELVETIA

Switzerland is bordered by France, Germany, Italy, Liechtenstein, and Austria; thus the country has four official languages: French, German, Italian, and Romansch (a descendant of Vulgar Latin spoken in the Swiss canton of Graubünden).

Statue of Helvetia on the Federal Palace of Switzerland in Bern.

Helvetia is the female personification of Switzerland. Like her counterparts Liberty (America; see no. 11), Marianne (France, no. 25), Italia (Italy), Britannia (Great Britain, no. 25), and Germania (Germany, no. 58), she represents the dreams and ideals of her country.

She derives her name from the Helvetii, an ancient tribe that inhabited the area occupied by modern-day Switzerland. In the early 1760s, the Helvetic society sought to unite the cantons by emphasizing Swiss nationalism and patriotism, a school of thought dubbed Helvetianism. In 1798 France invaded Switzerland and created the République Helvétique, essentially dissolving the cantons and imposing French Republicanism upon the Swiss people. The inability of the Swiss to create a national constitution led the French emperor, Napoleon, to abolish the Helvetic Republic in 1803. However, Helvetianism continued as a viable concept and eventually led to the creation of the Helvetian Confederation in 1848.

Helvetia first appeared on Swiss coins in 1850 in a seated position with her right arm outstretched toward the Swiss Alps in the background. Her left arm steadies a shield bearing the white cross of Switzerland on a red background. Switzerland had just become a confederation of individual cantons under the Swiss Constitution of 1848, and Helvetia was the perfect symbol for the new nation. The standing figure of Helvetia debuted in 1874 and has been a mainstay on Swiss half-franc, one-franc, and two-franc coins ever since, representing one of the longest tenures of the same female depiction on coinage. On some minor coins and on early gold coins, Helvetia is represented by the head of a young female with a crown, a laurel wreath, or braids. Several Shooting Festival 5-franc coins and medals feature Helvetia in a variety of depictions. On the Schaffhausen 5-franc piece of 1865, Helvetia appears with a young child. On the Bern 5-franc coin of 1885, she stands with her hand on the shoulder of the Swiss bear. Helvetia makes an appearance on modern 5-franc commemorative coins, as well. One of the most impressive Helvetia coins is the 1925 Swiss 100-franc piece, a large coin containing just under a full ounce of gold.

Ready for battle, Helvetia and the Bear stand as potent symbols of Switzerland. The bear on the reverse is the heraldic symbol of the Swiss city of Bern.

COLLECTING DIFFICULTY

Easy. Swiss coins bearing an image of Helvetia are common and inexpensive. The best-quality coins are termed "Specimen" (the practical equivalent of U.S. Proof coins). These have tiny mintages yet can be purchased for just a small premium over regular-issue coins.

Queen Juliana ruled the kingdom of the Netherlands from 1948 to 1980. She was third in an unbroken line of Dutch queens that began with the regency of Emma of Waldeck-Pyrmont in 1890, followed by Juliana's mother, Wilhelmina, then Juliana, and finally, Juliana's daughter, Beatrix (no. 60 among the 100 Greatest Women on Coins).

Queen Juliana was born Juliana Louise Emma Marie Wilhelmina in April 1909, the only daughter of Queen Wilhelmina and Prince Henry. Wilhelmina suffered numerous miscarriages before and after Juliana's birth, leaving Juliana the only heir to the Orange-Nassau line. Juliana's education consisted primarily of home-schooling by tutors followed by a bachelor's degree in international law from the Leiden University, the oldest university in the Netherlands.

In 1937 Juliana married Prince Bernhard, a German aristocrat of the house of Lippe-Biesterfeld, and a figure who generated much controversy during their marriage because of his German background, extramarital affairs, illegitimate children, and corruption. During World War II, Princess Juliana took their two children to safety in Ottawa, Canada, where they remained until the end of the war. In 1948 Juliana became queen after Wilhelmina abdicated because of her poor health and the loss of the Dutch colony of Indonesia. Likewise, Juliana abdicated because of poor health on Queen's Day (her birthday), April 30, 1980. Her date of death at the age of 94 was exactly the same as her grandmother's—but 70 years apart.

The first Dutch coins bearing Queen Juliana's portrait appeared in 1950, two years after her ascension to the throne. Her image appeared on all circulating coins, from the cent to the 5-gulden piece, from 1950 to the year of her abdication, 1980. She also appeared on some quasi-commemorative 10-gulden coins issued in 1970 (with her mother, Wilhelmina) and in 1973, as well as on a 50-gulden coin of 1990, where she appears with three other Dutch queens in the form of stylized rocks. The Netherlands Antilles issued numerous circulating and commemorative coins featuring Juliana. Suriname, under Dutch control until 1975, issued one-gulden coins bearing her portrait in 1962 and 1966.

This portrait of Queen Juliana appeared unchanged on Dutch coins issued from 1950 to 1980.

COLLECTING DIFFICULTY

Easy. The Netherlands struck mass quantities of coins bearing Queen Juliana's portrait, thus they are very common today, inexpensive, and available in nice condition. Juliana coins from the Netherlands Antilles are equally common; the coins of Suriname are less so.

No. 62

QUEEN JULIANA

In 1979 author William Hoffman referred to Queen Juliana as the richest woman in the world, claiming she was worth more than $600 million at the time.

Queen Juliana circa 1981.

No. 63

NATIVE WOMAN

Paul Gauguin lived with Vincent van Gogh in the latter's Yellow House in Arles, France. Their relationship was stormy and Vincent cut off a piece of his ear the same day he had a confrontation with Gauguin.

The cover to Gauguin's *Noa Noa*.

"Native Woman" can refer to any indigenous female, but, in this case, it refers to a body of work by the artist, Paul Gauguin, produced from 1891 until his death, during the time he lived in Tahiti and the Marquesas Islands.

Gauguin is considered one of the greatest post-Impressionist artists, though his works were not as appreciated during his lifetime as they were after his death. From 1891 to 1893, Gauguin moved to Tahiti to escape civilized life. Unfortunately, Tahiti was not the idyllic paradise he envisioned; nonetheless, he enjoyed the atmosphere and the erotic pleasure in which he indulged himself. During his time in French Polynesia, Gauguin focused almost entirely on painting native women, a thematic shift he maintained until his death. While in Tahiti, he wrote *Noa Noa: The Tahitian Journal*, in which he described his life and some of the history of the Tahitian people and their land. Some of his more famous works during this time include the paintings *Woman of the Mango* (*Vahine no te Vi*, 1892), *By the Sea* (*Fatata ti Miti*, 1892), *Spirit of the Dead Watching* (*Manao Tupapau*, 1892), and *Woman Holding a Fruit* (*Eu haere ia oe*, 1893). His paintings of native women are known for their bright colors and sensuality.

After returning to Paris for a short time, Gauguin returned to Tahiti from 1895 to 1901. In 1897 he created one of his largest works, *Where Do We Come From? What Are We? Where Are We Going?*, a jumble of humanistic and religious symbolism mixed with native men and women. In 1901 Gauguin moved to the island of Hiva 'Oa in the Marquesas Islands, where he lived out the remaining two years of his life.

In 2003 France produced coins denominated at one-and-a-half and 20 euros, marking the 100th anniversary of Gauguin's death. The 20-euro gold coin reproduced part of his 1893 painting *Woman Holding a Fruit*. However, without the vibrant colors of the actual painting, the image on the coin falls flat.

This 2003 20-euro coin from France features Paul Gauguin's painting *Woman Holding a Fruit*.

COLLECTING DIFFICULTY

Easy. Both denominations of French euro coins can be found online with ease. The silver one-and-a-half euro is affordable, while the 20-euro coin runs more than $1,000.

No. 64

QUEEN ARSINOE II

Endogamy, or marrying close within the family, was a common practice among the Ptolemaic dynasty. The intermarriages and the similarity of names create a confusing mess for historians.

Arsinoe II lived from around 316 BC to roughly 260 or 268 BC. She was an early member of the Ptolemaic line of Egyptian rulers that stretched all the way from her father, Ptolemy I, to the tragic Queen Cleopatra VII (no. 4 among the 100 Greatest Women on Coins). Her life was a roller-coaster ride of multiple marriages, threats to her life, the murder of two of her sons, and political intrigue, yet she navigated all of these with boldness and determination. Eventually, she found herself in a period of peace and stability. In the end, she became a goddess to her people.

Arsinoe II was the daughter of Ptolemy I, one of Alexander the Great's generals, who received Egypt as his portion of the divided empire. Her mother was Berenice I, Ptolemy's third wife. As an Egyptian princess, Arsinoe's fate was to enter into an arranged marriage for political purposes. Thus, when she was 15 years old, she wed Lysimachus, king of Thrace, Asia Minor, and Macedonia. The couple had three boys. Following Lysimachus's death in 281 BC, Arsinoe entered into another political marriage by marrying her half-brother, Ptolemy Keraunos. After Ptolemy killed two of her sons, she fled to Alexandria, Egypt, where her brother, Ptolemy II Philadelphos, and her step-daughter, Arsinoe I (yes, it gets confusing), ruled. Ptolemy II exiled Arsinoe I and married his sister, Arsinoe II, in the first direct sibling marriage of Ptolemaic Egypt. She predeceased her husband, who deified her following her death sometime between 260 and 268 BC.

Ptolemy II lived until 246 BC, during which time he issued numerous coins and medals honoring Arsinoe II. She is seen most frequently on gold octodrachms where she is shown facing right, wearing a diadem and a veil. Two cornucopias appear on the reverse with the Greek legend *Arsinoe Wife of Philadelphos*. A run of silver decadrachms with similar designs is sequentially numbered from A to omega, AA to double omega, and AAA to triple gamma, making for an interesting collecting challenge.

Arsinoe II as she appears on a gold octodrachm of the Ptolemaic Kingdom circa 180–116 BC.

COLLECTING DIFFICULTY

Difficult. Coins and medals bearing the image of Arsinoe II are actually quite plentiful, but they are always expensive. The entry level for a decent Arsinoe coin is around $5,000, and the price jumps quickly based on condition and rarity.

A bust of Queen Arsinoe II, 3rd century BC.

No. 65

GOLDA MEIR

Upon becoming Israel's foreign minister in 1956, Golda changed her last name from Meyerson to the Hebrew name Meir, which means "to illuminate."

Golda Meir circa 1973.

Golda Meir was an influential Israeli politician and leader who served as the first female prime minister of Israel from 1969 to 1974. She was instrumental in the establishment of the state of Israel and was a signer of the Israeli Declaration of Independence in 1948.

She was born Golda Mabovitch in May 1898 in Kiev, Russia. In 1905 she moved to Milwaukee, Wisconsin, where her family ran a grocery store. In high school she became an active member of the Zionist movement. In 1917 she married Morris Meyerson, and four years later, the couple moved to a kibbutz in Palestine. Golda became active in politics and served as an emissary to the United States from 1932 to 1934. She raised unexpectedly large amounts of money to help establish Israel, and she received the first Israeli passport. From 1949 to 1974 she served in the Knesset, the national legislature of Israel, as minister of Labor, and as foreign minister before becoming prime minister in 1969. She led Israel during the massacre of Israeli athletes at the 1972 Olympics and during the 1973 Yom Kippur War. Following the war, she was cleared in an investigation into Israel's lack of preparation for the Arab attacks. Shortly after her party won in the elections of December 1973, a tired and deflated Golda Meir resigned as prime minister and retired from politics. She died in 1978 of lymphatic cancer.

In 1995 Israel issued a bimetallic 10 new sheqalim coin with an image of Golda Meir appearing as a silhouette among vertical, parallel lines. She also appears on an unusual 50-euro medallic coinage issued in Israel in 1996 (perhaps this was made to appeal to European collectors, as the euro was never a denomination in Israel). This coin shows a three-quarter profile of Golda Meir facing right, a map of the world in the background, an airliner in flight at upper right, and a menorah at lower right. Numerous Israeli medals bear her image, as do some Israeli stamps and banknotes.

This bimetallic Israeli 1995 10–new sheqalim coin features Golda Meir's portrait made of parallel lines.

COLLECTING DIFFICULTY

Easy. A nice mini-collection can be made of the numerous Golda Meir coins and medals.

From time immemorial, the most natural way for a mother to feed her newborn infant has been by breastfeeding. Back before the days of baby formula, bottles, and nipples made of latex, silicon, or rubber, mothers fed their babies themselves or hired a wet nurse to do the job. Today, women have many options when it comes to breastfeeding (or not), and there are many references that discuss the pros and cons of this natural method of feeding a child.

In America, mothers began migrating from breastfeeding to bottle-feeding in the late 1800s because of high infant-mortality rates due to poor nutrition. Doctors and scientists began promoting baby formulas as a means to ensure proper nutrition and to reduce the variability of breastfeeding. By the middle of the 20th century, bottle-feeding was the accepted norm for infant nutrition, and breastfeeding became passé. In recent decades, the percentage of infants being fed at the breast has increased due to the efforts of organizations such as the La Leche League and a desire by many women to take a more natural approach to childrearing.

In 1971 Poland issued a 10-zlotych proba (pattern coin) with an unusual, in-your-face design that showed a baby's face on one side of the coin attached to a woman's breast on the other. The coin was not made for mass circulation, but the unusually large (for a pattern coin) mintage of 51,000 pieces ensured its wide distribution. Poland also issued a 100-zlotych coin in 1985 on behalf of the Women's Memorial Hospital Center that featured a woman breastfeeding on the reverse. The country of Turkey promoted breastfeeding more than any other with a series of coins issued in 1976, 1978, and 1980. All of the coins shared the same design on the obverse, that of a mother breastfeeding an infant while reading a book. Denominations included the diminutive 5 kurus, 10 kurus, 50 kurus, 1 lira, 2-and-a-half liras, 5 liras, and 500 liras in both gold and silver. In 1979 Egypt joined the ranks of countries promoting breastfeeding with 1-piastre, 5-piastre, and 1-pound coins that featured an image of an ancient Egyptian mother breastfeeding a child on her lap. Even Vatican City produced a breastfeeding-themed 50-lire coin, in 1982.

This Turkish 5-lira coin of 1976 shows a relaxed mother breastfeeding her infant child and reading a book. This was one of numerous coins issued around the world to promote breastfeeding.

COLLECTING DIFFICULTY

Easy. Most of the coins described above are readily available and affordable. A nice topical collection could be built just around this single theme.

No. 66

MOTHER BREASTFEEDING

Each year, the Centers for Disease Control and Prevention issue Breastfeeding Report Cards. According to the 2014 report, the national average for American babies breastfeeding at birth was 79.2 percent.

A Mother Breastfeeding her Child, **etching by C. Lewis and E.H. Landseer.**

No. 67

"Girl With a Harp," by Ivan Mestrovic

The chairman of the committee charged with selecting the best coin design in 1927 was none other than the famed Irish poet W.B. Yeats.

A lovely woman plucking her harp.

Ivan Mestrovic, the famed Croatian sculptor, created the striking "Girl With a Harp" design in 1927 as a competitive entry for a new coinage for the Irish Free State. Mestrovic resided in the United States at the time, and, because of postal delays, his design failed to arrive in time for the judging. Despite strong support for the design, it remained unused for decades until 1965, when it was adopted as the seal of the Central Bank of Ireland.

The harp has been a symbol of Ireland for centuries. The first mention of the harp as a heraldic symbol of the king of Ireland was in the 13th century, when it appeared in a French roll of arms. There it was described as "D'azure a la harpe d'or," which translates in English to "A harp of gold on a field of blue." This describes exactly the present-day coat of arms of Ireland and the standard of the president of Ireland. The seal of the president of Ireland incorporates an Irish harp as the central design, with the word "Eire" ("Ireland") below.

In 2007 Ireland and Croatia produced silver coins bearing Mestrovic's design to commemorate its 80th birthday. Both coins feature the "Girl With a Harp" design along with Mestrovic's name and the years of his birth and date surrounding. On the Irish version, the reverse design is a stylized, four-leaf clover with two squares and two lobes forming the leaves. The date, 2007, appears in one lobe and a Hibernian harp in the other. The denomination, 15 euros, appears at the base of the reverse. The Croation version is nearly identical, the difference being that the date appears in one of the squares, the Croatian arms appear in the other, the denomination is 150 kuna, and the name "Republika Hrvatska" (Croatia) appears at the top of the reverse.

80 years late, Ivan Mestrovic's design finally made it onto this Irish 50-euro coin.

COLLECTING DIFFICULTY

Easy. Numerous examples of the Irish and Croatian "Girl With a Harp" coins can be found online. Prices vary but range from $75 to $100 for individual coins and $300 to $400 for the two-coin set.

No. 68

ALICE PAUL

Alice Paul's First Spouse coin is the only one in the entire series that makes no mention of the related presidency. Her only connection to Chester Arthur is that she was born in the last year of his presidential term.

Alice Paul was a radical feminist and a soldier for women's rights in the early part of the 20th century. She took over the legacy of Susan B. Anthony, Elizabeth Cady Stanton, and other suffragists, and was instrumental in convincing President Woodrow Wilson to support the 19th Amendment to the U.S. Constitution, which finally gave women the right to vote.

She was born Alice Stokes Paul in January 1885 in Moorestown, New Jersey. She was highly educated, earning a Bachelor of Arts in biology from Swarthmore College, a Master of Arts in sociology, a Ph.D. in economics from the University of Pennsylvania, and law degrees from the American University.

While in England from 1907 to 1910, Alice met the Pankhurst sisters, who introduced her to a radical brand of feminism she had never seen before. This, she decided, was what was needed in America. In 1913 she helped organize a Woman Suffrage march on the day before President-elect Wilson's inauguration. The march attracted hundreds of thousands of viewers and garnered national publicity as a result of heavy-handed police tactics in breaking up the parade.

Alice was arrested several times in her political career, and she used her treatment in prison to garner public attention and sympathy. One of her favored tactics was the hunger strike, which often led to her being force-fed. Alice and the suffragists never relented, and in 1918 the U.S. Congress took up an amendment that gave women the right to vote. In 1920 the 19th Amendment became the official law of the land.

In subsequent years, Alice continued to fight for women through the Equal Rights amendment and the Civil Rights Act of 1964.

Alice Paul appears on the 2012 First Spouse coin for Chester Arthur and on the associated First Spouse medal. She appears on the coin with a short haircut and a steady, almost defiant gaze, her head turned directly toward the viewer. The reverse depicts a suffragist on the march, with an American flag over her right shoulder and a banner sash that reads "Votes for Women."

Alice Paul appears on the front of the First Spouse coin for Chester Arthur's term as president. The word "Suffragist" appears in place of the normal reference to the president's years in office.

COLLECTING DIFFICULTY

Easy. The Alice Paul First Spouse coin is readily available, but the fact that it contains half an ounce of pure gold makes it inherently expensive.

Portrait of Alice Paul.

No. 69

AUDREY HEPBURN

In a 2010 survey by the *British Daily Mail* newspaper, Audrey Hepburn in *Breakfast at Tiffany's* topped the women's list of their top five favorite film stars, but failed to make the men's list.

Audrey Hepburn, one of the most memorable film actresses of the 20th century.

Audrey Hepburn was a British actress who played in memorable films such as *Roman Holiday* (1953), *Sabrina* (1954), *Funny Face* (1957), *Breakfast at Tiffany's* (1961), *My Fair Lady* (1964), and many others. She was not only beautiful and stylish, but she had a heart of gold as well—she was active in UNICEF (shortened from United Nations International Children's Emergency Fund) from 1988 until her death in 1993.

She was born Audrey Kathleen Ruston in May 1929 in Brussels, Belgium, the daughter of a British father and a Dutch mother. From 1939 to 1945, Audrey lived with her mother in Arnhem in the Netherlands, where they suffered under the German occupation. Nevertheless, during that time she became proficient at ballet, a talent she would eventually use in the film *Funny Face*. Her memories of the deprivations during World War II inspired her later work in war-torn Somalia.

After World War II, Audrey continued to study ballet but was told she was too short (five foot seven inches) and too frail. She turned to acting and appeared in minor roles in some 1951 films. Her big break came when she appeared on Broadway in *Gigi*. In 1953 she beat out Elizabeth Taylor for the lead role in *Roman Holiday*.

In 1954 Audrey met and married Mel Ferrer, with whom she had a son in 1960 named Sean (in 2003 Sean published a moving pictorial tribute to his mother). Later in 1960, she starred in *Breakfast at Tiffany's*, arguably her most memorable film role. In 1964 she starred in *My Fair Lady*, but she complained later that most of her singing had been dubbed. After 1967 Audrey began winding down her film career, and in 1988 she shifted gears completely to focus on her humanitarian work.

She died in 1993 of abdominal cancer.

In 1994 and 1995, France produced a variety of silver and gold coins to commemorate the 100th anniversary of cinema, including coins featuring a three-quarter profile of Audrey Hepburn. In 1996 Gibraltar followed up with its own centennial celebration and created a copper-nickel one-crown coin with Audrey and her life and death dates on the obverse.

Audrey Hepburn graces the front of this massive, five-ounce gold coin struck to celebrate the 100th anniversary of cinema.

COLLECTING DIFFICULTY

Easy. Any of the copper-nickel or silver Audrey Hepburn coins is affordable and easily obtained. The gold versions are much rarer. France made 3,000 of the one-ounce Hepburn gold coins but only 99 of the five-ounce edition.

No. 70

QUEEN BERENICE II

According to the Greek poet Callimachus, Berenice sacrificed a lock of her long hair which became the constellation *Coma Berenice*, located near Bootes the Herdsman and his two dogs, Asterion and Chara.

Berenice II was one of the most formidable queens of the Ptolemaic dynasty, the successors of Alexander the Great. She was immortalized in Greek and Latin poems. She murdered one of her husbands and was murdered by one of her sons. She is scarcely known in written historical records, but she is well-known on the coins of her time.

Berenice II was the only daughter of Magas, the Macedonian king of Cyrene, and his wife, Apame, a princess of the Seleucid Kingdom. Berenice was born in Cyrene, a city in modern-day Libya, around 266 or 267 BC. In the 270s BC, King Magas attempted to invade Egypt but failed. To protect his kingdom from retaliation, he promised Berenice to the king of Egypt's son, but Magas died before the wedding took place. Apame repudiated the engagement and instead arranged a marriage between Berenice and Demetrius the Fair, a Macedonian prince. Whether the two ever married is unclear, but what is clear is that Berenice's mother and Demetrius became lovers. On Berenice's orders, assassins killed Demetrius in her mother's bedroom but spared her mother. Ultimately, Berenice married Ptolemy III Euergertes I, another son of the Egyptian king.

Berenice and Ptolemy III had six children in seven years. The couple enjoyed cult status in Egypt, expanded their influence abroad, built and restored temples, and saved their people from starvation twice when the grain crops failed.

Ptolemy III died in 222 BC, after which their son, Ptolemy IV, became ruler. To protect his position, Ptolemy IV murdered his uncle and his younger brother; for unknown reasons, he also killed his mother.

Berenice can be seen on bronze, silver, and gold coins of Ptolemaic Egypt. On gold octadrachms, Berenice's appearance is nearly identical to that of Arsinoe II (see no. 64), but their names on the reverse identify them clearly. Both ladies also feature cornucopias on the reverse, though Berenice's are usually single, while Arsinoe's are double. Occasionally, laureate caps of the Dioscuri flank Berenice's cornucopia; sometimes a bee is added to the reverse.

A veiled Berenice II appears on the obverse of this octadrachm from Ephesus, circa 241 BC. Her name appears in Greek letters on the left side of the reverse.

COLLECTING DIFFICULTY

Moderate. All coins bearing Berenice's portrait are scarce to rare. Low-grade bronze coins can be found for less than $200; silver versions are $800 and up; and gold versions sell for $7,500 and more.

***Queen Berenice II*, by Bernardo Strozzi.**

No. 71

SAINT ELIZABETH OF HUNGARY

Elizabeth was canonized as a Catholic saint in 1235, in part because of miracles attributed to her. One such miracle was the Miracle of the Roses. One day, while carrying loaves of bread in her cloak to feed the poor, Elizabeth encountered her husband, Louis, who insisted she open her cloak to prove to his companions that she was not stealing treasure from the castle. When she opened her cloak, white and red roses appeared in place of the bread.

The Charity of Saint Elizabeth of Hungary, by Edmund Leighton, circa 1895.

Saint Elizabeth was a princess of Hungary and, later, a duchess of Thuringia (part of Germany), she is famous for her charity and love for the poor. She lived a short life of only 24 years, but she is revered as a Catholic saint. The Elisabethkirche (Elizabeth Church) in Marburg is named after her.

Elizabeth was born in 1207 to King Andrew II of Hungary and Queen Gertrude of Merania. Her parents betrothed her to Louis IV of Thuringia in a marriage arranged for political reasons. Elizabeth and Louis married when she was 14 years old. She was influenced by Francis of Assisi, who was her contemporary and who corresponded with her before his death. She ministered to the poor by feeding them, clothing them, building a hospital, and attending to their needs.

Six years into their marriage, Louis died on his way to a crusade. Elizabeth's son, Hermann, was too young to become king, so Heinrich Raspe, Louis's brother, became regent for the boy. Elizabeth entered a life of celibacy under the influence of her priest-confessor, Konrad von Marburg, who also induced her to send her three children away. She continued serving the sick and the poor up until her death in 1231.

In 2007 Hungary issued a silver 5,000-forint coin to commemorate the 800th anniversary of Saint Elizabeth's birth. One side of the coin shows her as a nun feeding the poor; the other depicts her as queen, with roses and bread rolls in her lap, evocative of the Miracle of the Roses. Germany honored Saint Elizabeth with a silver 20-euro coin in 2007. On the reverse, she is shown standing with a pitcher in her right hand (viewer's left) and a roll of bread in the other. Surrounding her are a small castle, a church, and two indigents receiving food. The edge reads: *Wir Sollen die Menschen Froh Machen* ("We should make mankind happy").

Saint Elizabeth appears twice on this 2007 Hungarian 5,000 forint. The obverse of the coin portrays her Miracle of the Roses; the reverse of the coin shows her feeding the poor.

COLLECTING DIFFICULTY

Easy. The German Saint Elizabeth coin can be found with relative ease at prices ranging from $25 to $50. The Hungarian coin is a little more difficult to find, partly because the mintage is so low (only 4,000 each of the Uncirculated and Proof versions), and they run between $75 and $100 each.

No. 72

EVITA PERÓN

Evita is buried in the Duarte mausoleum in the La Recoleta cemetery of Buenos Aires, site of some of the most elaborate tombs in the world. For 16 years, her body went missing under the military dictatorship that replaced her husband.

Evita Perón was First Lady of Argentina from 1946 until her untimely death from cancer in 1952. She has achieved cult-like status in the decades since her death, in large part because of the work of her Eva Perón Foundation and her support of women's suffrage in Argentina.

The particulars of Evita's birth are unknown because of conflicting dates and names on her birth certificate and baptismal documents. There is no doubt that her parents were Juan Duarte and Juana Ibarguren, but the exact nature of their relationship was unclear, which may have led to the confusion or suppression of the facts.

Evita grew up in relative poverty in Junin, Argentina. In 1934 she moved to Buenos Aires where she worked as a model and an actress in film and on radio. In 1942, through her radio work, Evita met Juan Perón, then a colonel in the Argentine army. They married in 1945 and Juan became president of Argentina in 1946. Evita considered running for vice president of Argentina. She had the support of millions of working people, but not the military, who would have opposed her becoming president were Juan Perón to die (he was 24 years her senior). Ultimately, she decided not to run. In 1950 Evita was diagnosed with cervical cancer. Despite treatments and surgeries, the cancer ravaged her body, and by 1952 she was dead. She was accorded a state funeral which brought millions of her fans into the streets of Buenos Aires.

Evita did not appear on Argentinean coins until 1997, when the country used her image to commemorate the 50th anniversary of the Women's Suffrage Law. In 2002 Argentina honored her again on a silver peso and a copper-nickel two–peso coin on the occasion of the 50th anniversary of her death—the obverse of the coins features a bust of Perón facing left; the reverse shows the massive crowd that attended her funeral.

In 2002 Argentina commemorated the 50th anniversary of Evita Perón's death with this limited-edition silver peso. The crowd on the back represents the millions of people who mourned her death in 1952.

COLLECTING DIFFICULTY

Easy. Most of the coins that bear Evita's portrait were made for mass circulation, thus they are easy to obtain and inexpensive.

Evita with her husband, Juan Domingo Perón, 1950.

No. 73

THE RUSSIAN ROYAL FAMILY

In 1828 King Ludwig I of Bavaria issued a "Family Rouble" that appears strikingly similar to, and may have inspired, the Russian version.

Empress Alexandra Feodorovna, by A. Malyukov, circa 1836.

The Russian royal family of Emperor Nicholas I appears on the reverse of silver one-and-a-half-rouble coins dated 1835 and 1836. The obverses of the coins feature a large bust of Nicholas facing right. On the reverses, Empress Alexandra Feodorovna (formerly Princess Charlotte of Prussia) is surrounded by her seven children: Alexander II, Maria, Olga, Alexandra, Konstantin, Nicholas, and Michael. In 1835 the eldest child, Alexander II, turned 17 years old, and the youngest, Michael, turned three years old.

Empress Alexandra was born Princess Frederica Louis Charlotte Wilhelmina of Prussia in July 1798 to Frederick William III, king of Prussia, and Louise of Mecklenburg-Strelitz. In a politically motivated arrangement, Charlotte was promised in 1814 to Nicholas Pavlovich of Russia. The couple married in 1817 and settled in, never thinking that Nicholas might ever become emperor (he was third in line after his brothers Alexander I and Konstantin Pavlovich). However, when Alexander died in 1825 and Konstantin refused the throne, Nicholas became the unexpected emperor. By 1835, when the "Family Roubles" first appeared, Alexandra had already given birth to 11 children, four of whom either were stillborn or died in infancy. Alexandra was often ill, perhaps in part because of the rigors of her pregnancies, and she almost died in 1854. However, it was Nicholas who died first—of influenza—in 1855, predeceasing his wife by five years.

Their son, Alexander II (the young man at the top of the "Family Rouble"), became emperor of Russia upon his father's death. Maria became the duchess of Leuchtenberg (of Germany) but remained in Russia. Olga became the queen of Württemberg (also of Germany). Alexandra became a princess of Hesse (of Germany again) but died before moving there. Konstantin became an admiral in the Russian Navy. Nicholas became a field marshal in the Russian Army. Michael served as governor general of Caucasia.

Nicholas I's devotion to his wife and family is evident in this "Family Rouble" issued circa 1835. On the reverse of the coin, Empress Alexandra's seven children surround her.

COLLECTING DIFFICULTY

Extremely difficult. There are five different types of the Russian Royal Family one-and-a-half roubles, all of which are exceedingly rare. On top of that, Russian coins have exploded in value in the past two decades, putting them out of reach of most collectors. The entry level for any of these rarities appears to be around $50,000, if not more.

No. 74

CLARA SCHUMANN

Clara's fame as a musician never reached the level of her husband's, in part because as a female her music was less respected and, in part, because composers generally trump technicians in the musical field. Nonetheless, in their marriage Clara's virtuoso piano playing generated more income than Robert's composing.

Clara Schumann was the wife of the German composer Robert Schumann. However, she was a brilliant musical genius in her own right. In fact, it was an eight-year-old Clara who so impressed the 17-year-old Schumann with her piano playing that he gave up his study of law to focus on music. She was a virtuoso piano player who performed throughout her life to great critical acclaim, often from some of the greatest musicians of her age.

Clara was born Clara Josephine Wieck in September 1819 in Leipzig, Saxony (part of Germany). She received musical training from her father, who enforced a strict regimen of learning and practicing every day. She started touring at age 11, where she caught the attention of the great German author and poet, Goethe, and Niccolò Paganini, the celebrated violin virtuoso from Italy. Later performances brought her wider fame.

Though Clara and Robert Schumann had known each other from a young age, and had presumably fallen in love with each other at some point, Robert waited until she was 18 to propose marriage. The couple had to sue her father, who refused to give his blessing to the marriage. Two years later, after receiving permission from the court, the couple married. Over the course of their marriage, Clara and Robert had eight children, but only four of them survived her. Robert spent the last two years of his life in a mental institution with severe depression before he died in 1856.

Clara Schumann's image is arguably one of the most difficult to locate among the 100 Greatest Women on Coins. Hopefully, she will receive the recognition she deserves on a coin design in the future. Even in the realm of medals, she is a rarity—the medal pictured here is the only one of its type that the author could find, and even it is a hybrid medal that crosses over into banknote territory.

Clara Schumann appears in an interesting combination of a miniature banknote on a medal.

COLLECTING DIFFICULTY

Moderate. Because there is no Clara Schumann–specific coin, the collector is left with nothing but a currency-inspired medal. Truly desperate collectors might consider the actual German 100-mark banknote of 1989, which bears a charming, colorful portrait of Clara.

Clara Schumann, wife of Robert Schumann, was a distinguished musician in her own right.

No. 75

INDIRA GANDHI

Indira's husband, Feroze Gandhi, was no relation of Mahatma Gandhi. Gandhi is a common name in certain areas and castes of India.

Portrait of Indira Gandhi, 1977.

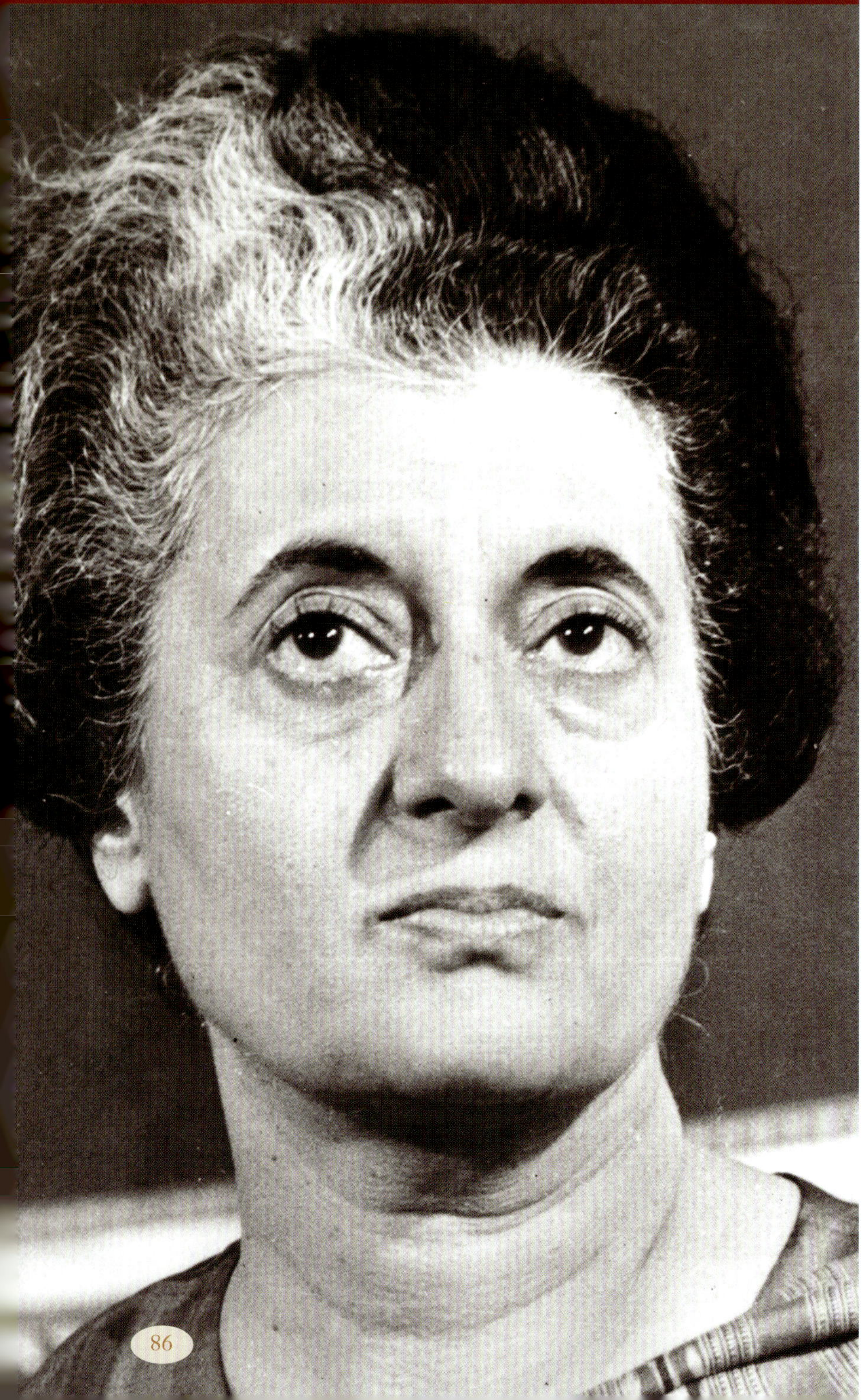

Indira Gandhi was prime minister of India from 1966 to 1977 and from 1980 to 1984, when one of her bodyguards killed her. She was the fifth prime minister of India and the only female ever to hold that position. She was a very strong, authoritarian leader who did much to improve the lot of poor people in her country.

Indira was born Indira Nehru in November 1917 in Allahabad, India, the only child of Jawaharlal and Kamala Nehru. The family was very wealthy, but her parent's involvement in Mahatma Gandhi's Indian independence movement caused a reversal of their fortunes. Her father and mother spent much time in and out of prison, creating substantial uncertainty in Indira's life. After numerous interruptions in her education, she travelled to England, where she studied for a time at Somerville College in Oxford (where Margaret Thatcher, no. 77, also attended). There she met her future husband, Feroze Gandhi.

Indira became prime minister of India in 1966 as the leader of the Congress Party. In 1971 she ran a successful anti-poverty campaign and began her second term as prime minister. She was stripped of her parliamentary seat in 1975 on a variety of charges of illegal campaign activities, but she remained in her post as prime minister, which led to civil unrest. The president invoked emergency powers, including unpopular curfews and censorship. In 1980 Indira's Congress Party won landslide victories, and she became prime minister again. In 1984 she quelled a Sikh rebellion in a brutal operation, which led two of her Sikh bodyguards to gun her down in retaliation on October 31.

In the year following Indira's death, India struck 50-paise, 5-rupee, 20-rupee, and 100-rupee coins in her honor. All of the coins feature a profile bust of Indira facing right; the reverse of each displays the Ashokan lions, the national symbol of India. The 100-rupee coin was made of 50 percent silver; the lower-denomination coins are made of copper-nickel. Indira Gandhi coins appear to be specific to India, as no others showed up in the survey of all world coins.

A profile bust of Indira Gandhi faces left on this Indian 5-rupee coin of 1985. Millions of Indians saw this coin because of its large mintage.

COLLECTING DIFFICULTY

Easy. The Indian 50-paise and 5-rupee coins are very common and cost less than $10 each. The 20-rupee and 100-rupee coins are not particularly rare, but they are difficult to locate and fetch anywhere from $125 to $200. Occasionally, coins in the original, governmental packaging are worth a premium—such is the case with the 100 rupee, where the packaging adds a 100 percent premium.

No. 76

LA PIETÀ, BY MICHELANGELO

Michelangelo was only 23 years old when he began sculpting La Pietà. The resulting work brought him international fame.

La Pietà is a large marble statue sculpted by the famous Italian artist Michelangelo (Buonarroti) between 1498 and 1499 AD. The statue depicts the Virgin Mary (no. 1 among the 100 Greatest Women on Coins) holding the limp, dead body of her son, Jesus, on her lap following his crucifixion. Both Mary and Jesus appear serene, leaving the viewer to imagine the intense sorrow and mourning felt by her (*pietà* means pity or compassion in Italian). The French Cardinal Jean de Bilhères commissioned the statue for his funeral monument in the Chapel of Santa Petronilla in Rome. However, the chapel was destroyed during the reconstruction of St. Peter's Basilica, beginning in 1506, and La Pietà was eventually moved to its present location just inside the Basilica.

Mary appears young in La Pietà, certainly younger than might be expected of a mother of a man in his 30s. Michelangelo made Mary's body out of proportion to that of Jesus to make the draping of his body appear more natural.

In 1972 geologist Laszlo Toth attacked the statue with a hammer, causing considerable damage to Mary's left arm (viewer's right), her nose, and one eye. Toth was never charged with a crime for his vandalism, but he was committed to an Italian psychiatric hospital. Restorers replaced Mary's arm, but because some visitors absconded with pieces of the broken statue, restorers used marble taken from the back of the statue to complete the restoration. Today, the statue is enclosed behind a clear, protective barrier.

In 1975 Nicaragua struck a gold 200-cordoba coin that featured an image of La Pietà. The outer legend reads: "Ayuda por construccion del hospital del niño" ("Help for the construction of the children's hospital"). Presumably, some of the proceeds from the sale of this coin helped defray the cost of the hospital; however, a search has failed to uncover to which hospital the coin refers or if the hospital was ever built. La Pietà also appears on a 1987 Vatican City aluminum 10-lira coin, which shows St. Peter's Basilica in the background. Numerous medals and tokens, which are sold primarily as souvenirs to tourists and collectors, feature La Pietà.

La Pietà is shown on this 1975 gold 200-cordoba coin of Nicaragua, with an appeal to help with the construction of a children's hospital.

COLLECTING DIFFICULTY

Easy. The least expensive version of a La Pietà coin is the 1987 Vatican City 10–lire piece, which can be obtained for less than $10. The gold Nicaraguan 200-cordoba coin is surprisingly affordable (less than $150) thanks to its small size, but it is difficult to locate. La Pietà medals and tokens are plentiful and can be found online with ease.

***La Pietà de Michelangelo,* in St. Peter's Basilica.**

No. 77

MARGARET THATCHER

Meryl Streep portrayed Margaret Thatcher in the 2012 movie *The Iron Lady*. The movie received mixed reviews, but Streep won a Best Actress Oscar for her performance.

The official photo of Margaret Thatcher, from the Margaret Thatcher Foundation.

Margaret Thatcher was the first female prime minister of the United Kingdom. She served for more than ten years, having won three consecutive elections and barely losing a fourth. She was dubbed the "Iron Lady" by Soviet journalists for her hard stance against Russian aggression.

Margaret was born in 1925 as Margaret Hilda Roberts, the second of two children of Alfred and Bethel Roberts. She acquired her taste for politics from her father, who was active in local politics in her birthplace of Grantham, Lincolnshire. She earned a Bachelor of Science degree in chemistry in 1947. While in college, she became active in Conservative politics. She ran for local office in 1950 and 1951 but lost both elections. It was during this time that she met Denis Thatcher, whom she married after a short courtship and with whom she had twins in 1953.

While continuing to seek political office, Margaret Thatcher also found time to earn a law degree and become a barrister. She won her first election in 1958 and became a member of parliament in 1959. She served as secretary of State for education and science from 1970 to 1974, during which time she cut funding for free milk for schoolchildren, leading to a predictable backlash. From 1975 to 1979 she led the minority Conservative Party in opposition to the majority Labour Party. From 1979 to 1990, she served as prime minister.

Highlights of her tenure include the successful Falkland Islands War, the breaking of the miners' strike in 1985, the privatization of national industries, the Sino-British Joint Declaration of 1984 (which dealt with Britain's eventual handing over of Hong Kong to China), and the end of the Cold War.

Margaret Thatcher appears on at least two coins issued in 2013, the year of her death, by the Ascension Islands and, appropriately, the Falkland Islands. She appears on numerous privately made medals, including rectangular silver ingots and gold-plated memorial medals, often with her "Iron Lady" nickname.

The Falkland Islands issued this crown in honor of Margaret Thatcher, the "Iron Lady," in the year of her death.

COLLECTING DIFFICULTY

Easy. Both the Ascensions Islands and Falkland Islands memorial coins are easily obtained and affordable (Uncirculated versions start at $25 and Proofs sell for slightly more than $100). The existence of numerous Thatcher medals makes the possibility of a mini-collection a viable proposition.

No. 78

QUEEN OLYMPIAS

In the 2004 movie *Alexander*, Angelina Jolie played the part of Olympias.

Olympias was the wife of King Philip II of Macedonia and the mother of Alexander the Great.

She was born Polyxena sometime around 375 BC to Neoptolemus, king of the Molossians (part of modern-day Greece). Later, she changed her name to Myrtale, allegedly as part of a cult initiation. Her marriage to Philip II was arranged by her uncle, Arymbas, who sought an alliance between the Molossians and the Macedonians. Myrtale received the name Olympias following Philip's victory in the Olympic games in 356 BC. In that same year, she gave birth to her son, Alexander. They also had a daughter, Cleopatra (no relation to any of the other Cleopatras in this book). At Cleopatra's wedding in 336 BC, one of Philip's own bodyguards assassinated him. Olympia, who was estranged from Philip at the time, was suspected of plotting his death—a natural assumption about a woman seeking to elevate her son.

In 1902 a hoard of gold medallions and coins was discovered in Aboukir, Egypt. Five of the medallions featured portraits of Olympias, including the one illustrated here. Olympias, with her head veiled, faces left with a scepter in her right hand. The reverse of the medallion depicts a Nereid, or sea nymph, riding a hippocampus, a mythological sea creature. On another of the medallions, Olympias is shown facing right, this time without a scepter; the reverse shows a Nereid riding a sea-centaur who holds a trident over his shoulder. These medallions may have been Olympic prizes or gifts for high officials.

Olympias also appears on smaller medals where her portrait is similar to the one illustrated here, but the reverse shows Alexander seated with a shield and helmet in the field. Another medal of the Roman emperor Caracalla (188 to 217 BC) shows Olympias reclining in bed with a snake (Olympias was a member of the cult of Dionysus, whose symbols included bulls and serpents, leading the famous Greek historian Plutarch to claim that, as part of her cult rites, Olympias slept with snakes).

Olympias is shown holding a scepter on the 58-mm gold medal from the Staatlichen Museen zu Berlin (Berlin State Museum). The reverse shows a Neried (sea nymph) riding on a hippocampus.

COLLECTING DIFFICULTY

Difficult. Coins or medals with portraits of Olympias are rare, and auction records are few and far between. One of the gold medals similar to the one illustrated here was offered at auction in 1972 for an estimate of 120,000 Swiss francs. A search of online archives shows a smaller, base-metal Olympias contorniate medal selling at around 1,100 euros.

***Cassandre et Olympias*, by Jean-Joseph Taillasson.**

No. 79

ARETHUSA

On some of the later tetradrachms, the artist ΚΙΩΟΝ placed his name on Arethusa's headband, though it can only be read on high-grade and well-struck examples. The center of the Arethusa fountain in Ortigia contains one of the only stands of wild papyrus in all of Europe.

Painting of Arethusa by Benjamin West, 1802.

In Greek mythology, Arethusa was a nymph who caught the attention of the river god, Alpheus, while bathing in his waters. Uninterested in his attentions, she sought protection from Artemis, the Greek goddess of the hunt. Artemis hid her in a cloud, but Arethusa became fearful and perspired so much that she turned into a stream. Artemis opened the earth to allow Arethusa to escape and she became an underground stream, but Alpheus pursued her out to the sea, where their waters mingled. They came up together on the island of Ortigia in a freshwater fountain that exists today, right on the edge of the sea. The fountain is on the western part of Ortigia, which is in the city of Syracuse in Sicily, Italy.

Arethusa has appeared on both ancient and modern coins. From ancient times, she is found on silver tetradrachms (four drachmas) and decadrachms (10 drachmas) of Syracuse from around 500 to 400 BC. Her portraits fall into several themes. In one she is shown facing nearly head-on with long, flowing tresses. In another she is shown in profile, with dolphins swimming around her head. Earlier renditions of this style show a more primitive head, also amid swimming dolphins. On the earliest versions, Arethusa appears as a small head within a quartered, incuse square that is eerily reminiscent of a swastika. One of the most interesting pieces is a small litra from around 405 BC, which shows Arethusa on the obverse of the coin and a wonderful image of an octopus on the reverse.

In modern times, Arethusa can be seen on a 1998 crown issued by Gibraltar. In 1873 the German town of Bad Fischau struck a bronze medal which borrowed heavily from the themes on ancient Arethusan coins. Her head appears on the obverse with scaly fish on either side instead of the ubiquitous dolphins; the reverse shows Nike hovering over a driver of a quadriga (a four-horse chariot).

Arethusa appears on the front of this Sicilian decadrachm wearing a triple pendant earring, a necklace, and a wreath of reeds in her hair. The dolphins swimming around her head remind us that she is a water-nymph.

COLLECTING DIFFICULTY

Easy or difficult. "Easy" refers to the modern coins; "difficult" refers to the ancient Arethusan coins, which are among some of the most popular of all ancient coins because of their lovely design. Well-heeled collectors might consider obtaining as many different obverse types as possible, then combine them with the numerous, different reverse designs.

No. 80

ATHENA AND NIKE

The large statue of Athena once housed in the Parthenon in Athens, Greece, held a statue of Nike in her right hand. Athena was covered in 44 talents' weight (approximately 2,400 pounds) of removable gold plates. Author Samuel Eddy believes much of the gold came from melted-down coinage, and that the valuable statue was eventually hauled off by Emperor Theodosius II to be turned into coins for his reign.

Athena (no. 27 among the 100 Greatest Women on Coins) and Nike (no. 23) are two of the most important and ubiquitous Greek goddesses. They appear individually on myriad ancient Greek coins, but they also appear together in many cases. Athena seems to be the dominant goddess when the two are together; Nike is always smaller and, literally, fits in the palm of Athena's hand.

On ancient Macedonian and Greek coins of the third and fourth centuries BC, Athena and Nike appear on opposite sides of the same coin. Athena is shown wearing a helmet. A full figure of Nike is shown on the reverse, with large wings, holding a wreath in her outstretched right hand and a staff in the other. On coins of the third century, Athena and Nike move together to the reverse of the coin, and Nike usually appears as a small figure in Athena's hand. This depiction continues through the Roman Republic and well into the Roman Empire (though by then, the two goddesses would have been known as Minerva and Victory).

In a typical pose of the two goddesses, a seated Athena holds Nike in her outstretched right hand.

A close-up of Nike in Athena's hand.

COLLECTING DIFFICULTY

Easy to moderate. Bronze and silver coins bearing images of Athena and Nike together are fairly common and relatively inexpensive, especially considering their age. Gold coins are another story—they are quite valuable even if they are not all that rare.

Marble statue of Athena holding Nike in her right palm.

No. 81

JULIA MAESA

According to the historian Barbara Levick, Julia Maesa's name may have come from the Arab word *masa*, which translates to "walk with swinging gait."

Artist Barry Brown Jr.'s conception of Julia Maesa, for whom no life-like ancient portraits exist.

Julia Maesa was the grandmother of the Roman emperors Elagabulus and Severus Alexander. She was also the older sister of Julia Domna (see no. 49). She and her sister were two of the most important women in the history of Rome, and they wielded considerable influence both in life and after death.

Julia was born in Syria in May 165 AD. She married C. Julius Avitus Alexanius, a member of the equestrian service who rose through the ranks and eventually became a Roman senator and consul, requiring a move to Rome in 208. The couple had two daughters, Sohaemias and Mamea. Her sister, Julia Domna, was the mother of the Roman emperor Caracalla; thus when Domna received the title of *Mater patrie et senatus* (Mother of the Country and the Senate), the same title was later conferred on Julia Maesa. After Caracalla's murder and Domna's suicide, Julia Maesa returned to Syria, where she plotted against the new emperor, Macrinus, in favor of her grandson, Elagabulus (son of Sohaemias). Elagabulus turned out to be one of the worst Roman emperors, engaging in all sorts of excesses, including a shocking marriage to a Vestal Virgin, thus turning his grandmother against him. She tricked Elagabulus into appointing his cousin, Severus Alexander, as his heir. When the Praetorian Guard killed Elagabulus and his mother in 222, Severus Alexander became emperor, and, once again, Julia Maesa came to power. She died in 226, missing the assassination of Severus Alexander in 235.

Numerous coins of the Roman Empire bear the portrait of Julia Maesa, though the most common are the silver denarii. Usually she is shown with the honorary title *Augusta*, a name usually given to wives of emperors, but, in this case, given to her as the grandmother of the emperor. She is paired with a variety of different goddesses, including Fecunditas (Fertility), Pudicitia (Modesty), Pietas (Loyalty), Juno (Protector of the State), and others. Occasionally, Julia appears on bronze sestertii, but they are offered less frequently than the denarii. In very rare instances, she can be seen on gold aureii.

This Roman denarius depicts Julia Maesa as she appeared circa 220 or 222 AD. On the reverse, Fecunditas (the goddess of fertility) holds a cornucopia and extends her right hand to a small child.

COLLECTING DIFFICULTY

Easy. Silver denarii bearing Julia Maesa's portrait are quite common and surprisingly affordable ($100 and up). As already mentioned, the sestertii appear to be less common, but they are no more expensive than the denarii.

Johanna Spyri was a Swiss author who wrote numerous books for children, the most famous of which is *Heidi*, the story of a small orphan girl who brightens the lives of everyone around her. *Heidi* is set in the Swiss Alps, where Johanna lived as a girl, and in Frankfurt, Germany (possibly inspired by the city of Zurich, Switzerland, where Johanna lived as an adult). Johanna wrote *Heidi* in two parts in 1880, but they are usually combined together as one book.

Unfortunately, little is known of Johanna Spyri, despite the fame she earned from her literary works. In fact, less has been written about her than most of the women in this book. Johanna preferred anonymity, and the lack of source material makes it difficult to construct a comprehensive biography. Suffice it to say that Heidi is vastly more famous than her creator.

What is known of Johanna's early years came from a childhood friend, Anna Ulrich, who recorded her memories of growing up with Johanna. Johanna Spyri was born Johanna Louise Huesser in June 1827 in Hirzel, a small village approximately 10 miles south of Zurich, Switzerland. When Johanna was 25 years old, she married Bernhard Spyri, with whom she had one son. She published her first story, *A Note on Vrony's Grave*, in 1870, when she was already more than 40 years old.

In 2001 Switzerland struck a special silver 20-franc piece to mark the 100th anniversary of Johanna Spyri's death. The artist, Sylvia Goeschke, modeled the portrait after one of the more famous images of Johanna. Sylvia's rendering of Johanna has a crude, almost unfinished appearance, with lines and crosshatching appearing on her face, hair, and clothing. The reverse appears to be a facsimile of her handwriting. As an associated item, Switzerland struck a gold 50-franc coin with a simple yet elegant portrayal of Heidi running across a plain field alongside a goat. The reverse shows a stylized landscape representing the alpine meadows where Heidi lived with her grandfather.

Johanna Spyri appears in a stylized portrait on this Swiss 2001 20-franc silver coin. The artist's name, Sylvia Goeschke, can be seen on Spyri's shoulder.

COLLECTING DIFFICULTY

Easy to moderately difficult. The Swiss 20-franc coin bearing Johanna's portrait is relatively inexpensive and easy to obtain. Uncirculated versions cost from $30 to $40; Proof versions run from $50 to $75. The "Heidi" 50-franc coin is a little more elusive because of its small mintage, and it is more expensive because it contains almost a third of an ounce of pure gold. Available only in Proof, the 50-franc coin rarely appears on the market and would probably bring $700 to $1,000.

No. 82

JOHANNA SPYRI

Several of Johanna Spyri's books, including *Heidi* and *Heimatlos* (Homeless), were styled as "Stories about children and for those who love children." Reportedly, Johanna wrote *Heidi* in four weeks.

Photo of Johanna Spyri by Johannes Ganz.

No. 83

LIVIA DRUSILLA (JULIA AUGUSTA)

Octavian's will made Livia an adopted member of the Julio-Claudian family and conferred the title of Augusta upon her, she being the first woman to receive that honor. Thereafter, her name became Julia Augusta. She received one-third of Octavian's considerable estate, allowing her to live quite comfortably until her death in 29 AD at the age of 87 (give or take).

Bust of Livia Drusilla, circa 31 BC.

In Roman history, Livia Drusilla stands out as one of the most important and influential women. She married the founder of the Roman Empire, Octavian, and was the grand matriarch of four generations of subsequent emperors: Tiberius, Claudius, Caligula, and Nero. Though portrayed on Roman coins, statuary, and portraits as a virtuous woman, she had a reputation as a political schemer who wielded considerable power over Octavian and who attempted the same with her son, Tiberius.

Livia was born in either 58 or 59 BC, the daughter of Marcus Livius Drusus Claudinius and Aufidia. Little of her youth is recorded, but around 43 BC she married her cousin, Tiberius Claudius Nero, a Roman patrician, with whom she had a son, Tiberius, in 42 BC. Following the assassination of Julius Caesar, the triumvirate of Octavian, Marcus Aemilius Lepidus, and Mark Antony banished Livia and her husband from Rome. Upon the restoration of peace, Livia returned to Rome, where she met Emperor Octavian in 39 BC. Octavian, already married, was so smitten by Livia that he divorced his wife and forced Livia and her husband to break up so that he could marry her. Livia and Octavian married in 37 BC and stayed together until his death in 14 AD—a marriage of more than 50 years. Following Octavian's death, Livia's relationship with her son, the new emperor, Tiberius, deteriorated to the point where he prevented or stripped most of her titles. Several years after her death in 29 AD, Livia's grandson, the emperor Claudius, restored her reputation.

Portraits of Livia on Roman coins are quite common. She appears most frequently on bronze dupondii (half sestertii), usually with an honorific title such as Salus Augusta (Safety), Pietas (Compassion), or Justitia (Justice). Tiberius included her portrait on several of his coins—in one instance, she and her son face each other on the front of a bronze provincial coin from circa 30 AD. On some of the silver denarii and gold aurei of Octavian and Tiberius, Livia appears on the reverse as the seated figure Pax (Peace).

Livia appears as Salus (the goddess of safety and well-being) on the front of this bronze Roman dupondius from 22 or 23 AD.

COLLECTING DIFFICULTY

Easy. Ancient Livian coins are plentiful and affordable. Decent bronze sestertii and silver denarii with Livia as Pax start around $200 each. Gold aurei of Tiberius with Livia as Pax are very rare, and acceptable examples will cost at least $3,000 each (better examples get expensive very quickly).

No. 84

EMPRESS ELISABETH OF AUSTRIA

The Kaiserin-Elisabeth-Westbahnhof was renamed the Wien Westbahnhof in 1951. The statue of Elizabeth still stands in the main concourse, not far from a McCafé restaurant.

Elisabeth was the empress of Austria beginning in 1854 and queen of Hungary from 1867 until her assassination in 1898. She was known for her exceptional beauty, vanity, long hair, fits of melancholy and depression, and strict diet and exercise regimen.

She was born Elisabeth Amalie Eugenie in December 1837 to Duke Maximilian Joseph of Bavaria and Princess Ludovika. At the age of 15, she met the 23-year-old Emperor Franz Joseph of Austria, who was considering proposing to Elisabeth's older sister, Helene. He was more impressed with Elisabeth and chose her instead. Thus, on April 24, 1854, Elisabeth became the empress consort of Austria.

Elisabeth chafed under the rigidity of the Austrian court and escaped by indulging herself in various pursuits, including travelling for long periods of time, spending lavish amounts on beauty care and treatments, riding horses, and exercising for hours on end. Her fanaticism about her weight and waistline suggests a lifelong eating disorder. She suffered bouts of depression and was only well when she was away from her husband and the Austrian court. Her marriage produced four offspring, but, in later years, her relationship with Franz Joseph became more platonic.

On September 10, 1898, Luigi Lucheni, an Italian anarchist, plunged a sharpened file into Elisabeth's chest, puncturing her heart. The small size of the wound belied its seriousness; while there was little external blood, Elisabeth's heart continued leaking blood until it eventually stopped beating.

In 2008 Austria produced a 20-euro silver coin to commemorate the 150th anniversary of the opening of the Kaiserin-Elisabeth-Banhhof in Vienna. The reverse of the coin shows the statue of Empress Elisabeth on the station platform with a lady disembarking from a long train. The obverse shows the locomotive LOK kkStb 306, which was built in 1908. Elisabeth is portrayed on a gold ducat of 1867 on the occasion of her coronation as queen of Hungary. She is shown in profile facing right, her hair in a long braid beneath a crown and veil. In 1998 St. Thomas and Prince Island struck silver and gold versions of a 1,000-dobra coin to observe the 100th anniversary of Elisabeth's death.

Elisabeth of Austria as she appeared in 1867 on a gold ducat issued for her coronation as the queen of Hungary.

COLLECTING DIFFICULTY

Moderate. The 2008 Austrian 20-euro coin is not rare, but it appears for sale infrequently—perhaps because the coin saw wide distribution and it only comes on the market when collectors are ready to sell. Typical selling prices for this coin range from $75 to $100. Likewise, the 1867 Austrian gold ducat is scarce and rarely appears on the market. The author was able to find the St. Thomas and Prince Island coin only in online sites in Europe—the asking price on the silver Proof was 24.50 euros; the tiny gold versions ran from 48 to 65 euros.

Elisabeth, the murdered empress of Austria. Painting by Philip de László (1899).

No. 85

FAITH, HOPE, CHARITY, AND MOTHER SOPHIA

All of the Niue rectangular coins are slightly convex, an innovative technology that has been applied to coins only in recent years.

This painting of Faith, Hope, and Charity was produced by Karp Zolotaryov circa 1685.

Of all the stories in this book, this is perhaps the most tragic and horrific, even with the historical inconsistencies that are sometimes cited. It is the story of a mother, Sophia, who lived in the second century AD, and her daughters, Faith, Hope, and Charity. The names of the daughters derive from one of the apostle Paul's letters to the church at Corinth (I Corinthians 13:13), which reads, "But now abide faith, hope, and love...." Apparently, it was not uncommon for Christian parents to give their children virtues as names.

Sophia and her three girls lived in Italy during the reign of the Roman emperor Hadrian, who ruled from 117 to 138 AD. They made the fatal mistake of expressing their faith at a time when Christians were being persecuted in Rome. Someone exposed them to the authorities, and they were sent to Rome to receive punishment. Starting with the eldest daughter, each of the girls was tortured in the presence of the others to induce them to renounce their faith and worship the Roman goddess Artemis, which they each refused to do. After torturing the girls, the Romans beheaded each of them. Sophia's punishment was to witness her daughters being tortured and murdered, then to gather up their bodies and bury them on a hill outside the city. She remained beside their graves for three days before finally dying herself.

Sophia and her daughters appear in religious art and icons where their names are shown in Greek, Cyrillic, Latin, or English. Charity's name is sometimes shown as *Agape* (Greek for *love*).

Sophia and her three daughters appeared on the reverse of rectangular $2 "coins" issued by Niue in 2012 and 2014. The 2012 coin was made of pure silver overlaid with gilt decorations and colorized faces and hands. One version of the 2014 coin was oxidized in black, offsetting the colorized hand and faces of the four figures. A second version was identical except that the coin was gilt instead of being oxidized.

Mother Sophia and her three daughters appear on this unusual rectangular $2 coin from the island nation of Niue. The depiction is typical of Russian icons from the 17th and 18th centuries.

COLLECTING DIFFICULTY

Easy. The black oxidized version of the 2014 Niue coin can be found online for less than $100. The gilt 2014 versions sell frequently in the $100 to $150 range. The 2012 edition is the most difficult to find and rarely appears on the market.

Princess Gina was the wife and consort of Franz Joseph II, the prince of Liechtenstein, from the year of their marriage in 1943 until her death in 1989.

Gina was born Countess Georgine Norberte Johanna Franziska Antonie Marie Raphaela von Wilczek in October 1921 in Gratz (now Graz), Austria, the daughter of the count of Wilczek and the countess of Wchinitz and Tettau. At her marriage to Prince Franz Joseph II, she became known as Her Serene Highness the Princess of Liechtenstein. The line of Liechtenstein is hereditary and patriarchal, thus neither Gina nor her female heirs could be in line for succession.

Gina and Franz Joseph had five children, the eldest of whom was Prince Hans-Adam, the current ruler of Liechtenstein. Their only daughter was Princess Nora, the current Marquessa of Mariño. The family lived in a castle atop a hill adjacent to Vaduz, the capital city of Liechtenstein.

In 1945 Gina was one of the founders of the Liechtenstein Red Cross, and she served as its first president until 1985, when her daughter-in-law, Princess Marie, took over.

Gina died in October 1989, reportedly from cancer. She predeceased her husband, who was 15 years her senior, but he died less than a month later.

Gina appears on a 100-frank gold coin issued by Liechtenstein in 1952 and on 25- and 50-frank gold coins issued in 1956. On all three coins, Gina is shown with her husband as conjoined busts; hers is in the secondary position in the background. The author knows of no other coins that bear Gina's portrait.

Princess Gina appears with her husband, Franz Joseph II, on this scarce 100-frank gold coin issued by Liechtenstein in 1952.

COLLECTING DIFFICULTY

Moderate. The 1952 Liechtenstein gold coins bearing Gina's portrait have healthy mintages of 17,000 coins each, so they are not rare, but the fact that they are gold makes them automatically expensive. The 25-frank coin sells for $300 to $400; the 50-frank coin sells for $450 to $600. The 1956 100-frank gold coin has a much smaller mintage of only 4,000 pieces, thus it is more difficult to locate. Prices range from $1,600 to $4,000 depending on condition.

No. 86

PRINCESS GINA OF LIECHTENSTEIN

Liechtenstein is a tiny country tucked in the mountains between Switzerland and Austria. In 1868 Liechtenstein disbanded its military and has maintained a policy of neutrality ever since.

Anyone planning a trip to Liechtenstein should consider hiking the 12 kilometer (7.46 miles) Princess Gina Trail (Fürstin-Gina-Weg) that runs from the ski-resort village of Malbun to the top of the Augstenberg mountain at 2,359 meters (1.47 miles) elevation.

Princess Gina of Liechtenstein with husband Prince Franz Joseph II.

No. 87

INGRID BERGMAN

At one of Ingrid's first acting tryouts, the best candidates were given a white envelope, the worst, a brown envelope. When Ingrid took the stage for her tryout, the judges seemed disinterested and dismissed her abruptly after cutting her performance short. She left crushed, even contemplating suicide. After arriving home, she learned to her delight that a white envelope awaited her. Years later, one of the judges explained that they dismissed her early because they knew immediately that she was going to be a great actress.

Portrait taken of Ingrid Bergman in the 1940s.

Ingrid Bergman was a Swedish actress who found great success in Italian and American films, most notably in *Casablanca*, where she played Ilsa Lund, the wife of a Nazi resistance fighter during World War II. She was known for her natural beauty, her disdain for makeup, and the high level of professionalism she brought to acting.

She was born in August 1915 in Stockholm, Sweden, the daughter of a Swedish father and a German mother. Her mother died when she was 3 and her father died when she was 13. She bounced around with family members until she finally earned a place at the Royal Dramatic Theatre School at the age of 17. She left the school prematurely (after only one year) in order to act in Swedish films. She appeared in the Swedish film *Intermezzo* (1936), which brought her to the attention of American filmmakers, who cast her in an American remake of the film in 1939.

Ingrid appeared opposite Humphrey Bogart in *Casablanca* in 1942, in the midst of World War II. This was her most memorable role, though she won no acting awards for it. *Casablanca* was filmed in black-and-white; her first color film was the adaptation of Ernest Hemingway's *For Whom the Bell Tolls* (1943).

Her last film was *A Woman Called Golda*, in which she played the role of the late Golda Meir (no. 65 among the 100 Greatest Women on Coins), the former prime minister of Israel. Ingrid was ill with breast cancer throughout the filming and she died four months after the film's completion.

In 1996 Gibraltar issued a series of one-crown coins as part of their *Centenary of the Cinema* series. One of the coins features Ingrid Bergman along with Humphrey Bogart as they appeared in *Casablanca*.

Gibraltar honored Ingrid Bergman on this 1996 crown. Here she appears with her co-star, Humphrey Bogart, from the movie *Casablanca*.

COLLECTING DIFFICULTY

Moderate. The Gibraltar crown is not a rare or expensive coin, but it is surprisingly difficult to locate. In fact, though it only cost $14.99 once it was found, the copper-nickel version was the most difficult coin to hunt down for this book. In a six-month search, the author never saw the silver version for sale.

No. 88

UNA

The design on the Gibraltar coins shows the lion stepping on (or holding) a key. This is a justifiable alteration because the golden key is part of the seal of Gibraltar and symbolizes the territory's importance as a gateway to the Mediterranean.

Lady Una was a character in Edmund Spenser's *The Faerie Queene*, an epic poem from the Elizabethan era. Una represented Truth and the "true (Protestant) church." By extension, Una represented Queen Elizabeth I (see no. 18), for whom this poem was more-or-less intended. Spenser published the first part of *The Faerie Queene* (Books I–III) in 1590 and the second part (Books IV–VI) in 1596. Book VII, which is incomplete, appeared in 1609. Spenser wrote *The Faerie Queene* in a quaint, archaic English, even modifying and inventing words to give the poem a special character.

Una appears in Book I as she travels with the Redcross Knight, who represents England. She recruits the Redcross Knight to slay a dragon that is besieging her parents' castle. Along the way, she counsels the Knight as he struggles against the allegorical characters of Sloth, Despair, Error, Falseness, Duplicity, and Pride. While separated from the Knight, a lion rushes at her from the woods, fully intent on eating her, but the lion is amazed by her beauty, and, instead of killing her, he kisses her feet and licks her hands. Thereafter the lion remains her faithful companion, guarding her along her journey. At the end of Book I, Una is reunited with the Knight and marries him.

The first appearance of Una and the Lion on a coin was in 1837, when William Wyon created a design for a magnificent 5-pound gold coin with which to kick off Queen Victoria's reign. Wyon's design incorporated Queen Victoria as Una, which was a unique metamorphosis of a British ruler. Survivors are very rare and expensive because the total edition was limited to only 400 pieces. In 1989 Gibraltar commemorated the 150th anniversary of the design by resurrecting it for a gold 5-sovereign coin. In 1997 Gibraltar used the design again on a gold 2-pound coin, this time to celebrate the 200th anniversary of the first striking of coins for Queen Victoria.

Una and the Lion appear on the back of this British 5-pound gold coin of 1839, issued in the first year of Queen Victoria's reign. This design ranks high on the list of the world's most beautiful coins.

COLLECTING DIFFICULTY

Moderate to extremely difficult. The Gibraltar gold coins are elusive and expensive because of their small mintages and the gold they contain. The price of the British Una and the Lion gold coins starts at $50,000 and goes up depending on quality.

***Una and the Lion*, by Briton Riviere.**

No. 89

STRÓBL MONUMENT

The original plaque on the statue honored the Russian soldiers who liberated Hungary from the grips of the Germans in 1945. In later years, Hungary revolted against the Soviets, and, after Hungary became an independent republic in 1989, the plaque was changed to honor all those who helped Hungary gain its freedom. The statue remained the same, but changing political circumstances forced its reinterpretation.

The Liberty Statue on the Gellért Hill, Budapest, Hungary.

Erected in 1947, the Stróbl Monument, also known as the Liberty Statue (*Szabadság Szobor* in Hungarian) or Freedom Statue, is located in Budapest, Hungary. Zsigmond Kisfaludi Stróbl, the great Hungarian sculptor and artist, designed the statue. The pedestal upon which the statue stands is 26 meters (85.3 feet) high; the statue itself is 14 meters (44.9 feet) high. The statue stands on the top of Gellért Hill in central Budapest, on the west side of the Danube River. Because of its height, it can be seen from great distances, and visitors to the statue are treated to a commanding, panoramic view of the city. Two smaller bronze statues sit at either side of the base of the Liberty Statue. On one side is a partially clad male thrusting a torch into the wind; on the other side, a nude male is about to kill a two-headed dragon with a stone. The original complex included a statue of a Red Army soldier at the base of the Liberty Statue, but it was removed years later when Hungary earned its independence.

Several Hungarian coins feature the Stróbl Monument, including the 10-forint coin issued from 1971 to 1989 and the silver 50- and 100-forint coins struck only in 1970. Hungary struck the 10-forint coins for circulation, and their mintages ran as high as 37 million coins in a single year. The 50- and 100-forint coins commemorate the 25th anniversary of liberation from the Germans. Their mintages are much smaller (5,000 for the Proof strikes and 20,000 for the Uncirculated versions). All of the coins show Liberty holding aloft an oversized palm frond, but not the tall pedestal on which she stands.

This design of Liberty holding an oversized palm frond is from a statue in Budapest, Hungary. The coin shows only the bronze statue of Liberty and omits the tall pedestal that allows her to tower over her surroundings.

COLLECTING DIFFICULTY

Easy. The 10-forint coins are extremely common, which ironically may be problematic for collectors. Most dealers do not stock them, because of their low value. More interesting options are the silver 50- and 100-forint coins. Their low mintages and inexpensive prices seem like excellent values, plus they are part silver. Both can be found in the range of $15 to $25.

No. 90

YOUNG WOMAN WRITING

Upon its introduction in 1980, the Mozambique metical equaled one escudo from the old system. By 2004 the metical had become virtually worthless because of hyperinflation.

The "Young Woman Writing" appears on the first 1-metical coins of Mozambique under the reform coinage of 1980. The young woman appears to be a student writing in a notebook. All 1-metical coins since 1980 have borne the same obverse design, though they have been issued sporadically: 1980 to 1986, 1994, and 2006 (after which the denomination ceased).

What was the purpose of the design of a young woman writing? A look at the first reform coins of 1980 provides some answers, because the designs reflect the priorities of the Mozambique government. Each of the coins minted in 1980 includes the seal or emblem of Mozambique on the reverse. The emblem consists of a cog wheel (Industry) surrounded by ears of wheat and corn (Agriculture). In the center, a book (Education) appears in the background. In the foreground, a bayoneted rifle (Military) crosses a hoe (Agriculture, again). The obverses of the coins represent one of these themes. Thus, the young woman writing on the metical represents education. Similarly, the 1980 two-and-a-half-metical coin shows a crane and a ship, which represent industry. The tractor on the front of the 1980 5-metical coin represents agriculture, and the armored personnel carrier on the front of the 1980 20-metical coin represents the military. These are excellent examples of how designs on coins can be used to influence a population by reinforcing the country's values. Mozambique had a literacy rate of 56% in 2013, compared to a worldwide rate of 84.1%. Promoting education was vital for the country's future.

A driver of the low-literacy rate in Mozambique is a history of recent disruptions. In 1975 Mozambique won its independence from Portugal and immediately expelled all the Portuguese and confiscated their assets. From 1977 to 1992, Mozambique endured a civil war that displaced millions of people who fled the violence. After the end of the war, with stability restored, millions of people returned to their homes in one of the largest repatriations ever recorded. In 2002 a cyclone disrupted an already fragile infrastructure. Since 2004, AIDS has been on the rise in Mozambique, affecting hundreds of thousands of people.

The future will determine whether a young woman writing on a coin can make a difference in the face of all these obstacles.

This 1-metical coin of Mozambique shows a female student writing in a notebook.

COLLECTING DIFFICULTY

Easy. The 1-metical coins of Mozambique are very inexpensive and plentiful.

An engraving of poet Phillis Wheatley.

No. 91

ANGEL

The Christian angel may be an extension of the goddess Nike (see nos. 23 and 80), who was usually shown as a winged female hovering over the earth.

Angel bearing Veronica's Veil, by Cosimo Fancelli.

Angels are spiritual beings who fill the gap between humans and God. The purpose of angels, their appearance, and what they represent are all subject to incredible speculation, because, for the most part, what we know about them leaves plenty of room for interpretation. In the Christian Bible, angels perform several functions: messenger, God-worshipper, care-giver (or guardian), encourager, dispenser of justice. For example, in the story of Mary's (No. 1) miraculous conception, the angel Gabriel announced her impending pregnancy, and an unnamed angel explained to her fiancé, Joseph, how this was a good thing. In modern times, the concepts and roles of angels have expanded far beyond the religious realm into the secular world, where angels have been incorporated into astrology, magic, spiritual healing, and even witchcraft.

Angels can be good, angels can be bad, and even their appearance can change. In essence, angels can be anything the human mind can conjure. As a result, angels can become both believable and useful, or they can be reinterpreted into something they are not. For example, in the movie *Constantine*, the angel Gabriel (the same one who appeared to Mary) works against God and mankind.

On coins, angels make frequent appearances. The Isle of Man has an entire series of bullion coins called *Angels*. From 1871 to 1898, France produced 20-franc gold coins with a winged angel on the obverse. During the reign of King Henry VIII, England produced gold coins with an angel slaying a dragon. However, the angels on the aforementioned coins are all male, so the challenge for collectors is to find female angels. One such coin is the 2014 Niue Island "Guardian Angel" coin, which features a young girl angel with wings. Similarly, the British Virgin Islands produced a $5 coin in 2013 depicting a boy and girl angel in love. In 2012 Niue Island produced an unusual, star-shaped $2 Christmas coin with a small angel sitting on a crescent moon.

A young guardian angel is ready to protect the owner of this silver Niue Island $2 coin.

COLLECTING DIFFICULTY

Easy. Most of the modern coins depicting female angels can be found online for less than $100.

No. 92

EMPRESS CATHERINE I OF RUSSIA

Catherine was the first female ruler of Russia, but it was the efforts of Alexander Menshikov (the man who "gave" her to Peter years before) that cemented her succession.

Catherine I was the empress of Russia from 1725 to 1727 and, earlier, the empress consort of Russia from 1721 to 1725. Her life was a true rags-to-riches story. Unlike many of the queens, princesses, and empresses in this book, who were all carefully selected as wives for their kings, princes, and emperors, Catherine was of low birth, illiterate, and a mistress to others, including her own husband, before she ascended to one of the most powerful positions on the planet.

She was born Marta Elena Skavronska in either 1683 or 1684 and was the daughter of a gravedigger from the province of Livonia in Sweden and a woman whose name is uncertain. Marta's father died of the plaque when she was two, and her mother died in the same way the following year, leaving Marta an orphan to be raised by her aunt and uncle. In 1702 she was engaged to be married to a young Swedish soldier but was instead taken captive by an invading Russian army. She became the household servant of the general of the occupiers. Shortly thereafter she became the mistress of Alexander Menshikov, a friend of Tsar Peter I (Peter the Great), who eventually transferred Marta to the tsar as a means of gaining influence. After moving to Moscow, Marta gave birth to a boy in 1704, the first of 12 children by Peter. She received her new name, Catherine Alexeyevna, after being baptized into the Russian Orthodox Church. In 1711 Peter, though still married to his first wife, made Catherine his consort, essentially elevating her to the rank of tsarina. On February 9, 1712, Peter finally wed Catherine, and in 1724 he named her empress of Russia. When Peter died in 1725, Catherine ruled alone for three years until her death in 1727.

Because Catherine reigned for such a short period, she appears on only a limited number of Russian coins. Unlike her predecessors and successors, she never appeared on a coin with a face value below a half rouble. On gold coins, she only appeared on a 2-rouble piece.

Catherine I of Russia graces the front of this 2-rouble gold coin that was restruck sometime after 1726.

COLLECTING DIFFICULTY

Easy, but fairly expensive because of the extreme popularity of Russian coins. Low-grade roubles start at $500 and decent examples cost around $1,500.

***Catherine I*, by Jean-Marc Nattier, circa 1717.**

No. 93

MARILYN MONROE

Marilyn appeared in the first issue of *Playboy* magazine in December 1953 as the very first Playmate of the Month (then known as Sweetheart of the Month).

A young Marilyn Monroe smiles for a publicity photo in 1950.

Marilyn Monroe was a famous movie star of the 20th century, a sex symbol, an American icon, and a tragic, misunderstood figure. She is remembered for her beauty, her dumb-blond act (she was really quite bright), and her mysterious death in 1962.

She was born Norma Jeane Mortenson in June 1926, the daughter of Martin Edward Mortenson and Gladys Baker. Martin left Gladys shortly before Marilyn's birth and was never a part of her life. Gladys suffered severe mental problems and was hospitalized for much of her adult life, leaving Marilyn in a succession of foster homes and adoptive families. When she was 16, Marilyn married James Dougherty but divorced him four years later. Her second marriage, to baseball legend Joe DiMaggio, lasted only six months. In 1956 she married playwright Arthur Miller, but that marriage ended in 1961. In August 1962, Marilyn's psychiatrist found her dead from an overdose of barbiturates in an apparent suicide.

Her first big acting break came in John Huston's 1950 film, *The Asphalt Jungle*. Other notable films included: *Niagara* (1953), *Gentlemen Prefer Blondes* (1953), *The Seven Year Itch* (1955), *Some Like It Hot* (1959), *Bus Stop* (1956), and *The Misfits* (1961).

Despite her successful film career, Marilyn was very insecure and suffered from severe stage fright. In later years, as she descended into drug addiction and depression, she became increasingly difficult to work with, leading to her being fired from her last film. Despite the commercial success of several of her films, she never won an Oscar for any of her performances.

In 2011 the Cook Islands produced a Marilyn Monroe $5 coin in commemoration of the 85th anniversary of her birth. The reverse of the coin features three different images of Marilyn, all colorized, including a central portrait with a diamond chip set into the coin as an earring. Also in 2011, the Cook Islands produced a $5 coin featuring Bruno Bernard's famous photograph of Marilyn standing above a steam grate, her dress billowing upwards. In 2013 Marilyn appeared on another Cook Islands coin, this time a gold-plated $1 *Hollywood Legends* coin.

Notice the diamond earring Marilyn Monroe wears on this special commemorative $5 coin issued by the Cook Islands in 2011.

COLLECTING DIFFICULTY

Easy. Any of the Cook Islands coins described above are readily available on the Internet anywhere from $50 to $100. The Bruno Bernard coin may be difficult to locate as an individual because it was sold originally as part of a six-coin set.

No. 94

THE SLEEPING BATHER, BY RENOIR

Probably intentional, the mintage of *The Sleeping Bather* coin matches exactly the year it was painted: 1,897.

The Sleeping Bather (or *The Sleeper*) was painted by Pierre-Auguste Renoir in 1897. It is a remarkable painting because Renoir completed it at a time when his rheumatoid arthritis was well advanced, and he had great difficulty even holding a brush. The painting shows a nude woman with a thin dress draped decorously across her lap, relaxing and sleeping after her bath.

Throughout his career, Renoir painted numerous nudes, though they were not the primary focus of his works. He completed his earliest nudes while working in a porcelain factory prior to 1861, where he painted female forms on vases in addition to the usual floral designs, birds, and other decorative motifs. After hours, he copied the works of the masters in the Louvre, which included nudes by Peter Paul Rubens and others. In 1867 he painted *Diana*, a depiction of the goddess of the hunt almost completely nude, unstringing her bow after having killed a deer. One of his first Impressionist paintings was his *Nymph at the Stream* from 1869 or 1870, which shows a nude female lying on a bed of moss. In 1870 he painted *Bather*, a nude woman standing next to her clothing and a pet dog. This was one of two paintings Renoir sent to the Paris Salon of 1870. His 1880 *Little Blue Nude* shows a young woman holding her ankle. While visiting Naples, Italy, in 1881, Renoir painted the first version of his *Blond Bather*, which shows a young nude woman with blond hair set against a background of blue, yellow, and green pastels. A second version painted in 1882 features subtle differences and variations in the background. Renoir's 1885 *Bather Arranging Her Hair* puts the focus on the back of a nude woman and on her dark hair. In 1886 Renoir shifted stylistically and began to focus more and more on nudes, which became more frequent themes in his work even as late as 1919, the year of his death.

In 2012 the Cook Islands produced a colorized, three-ounce silver coin of $20 face value featuring an image of Renoir's *The Sleeping Bather*. This was part of a 20-coin series entitled *Masterpieces of Art* issued between 2008 and 2013.

For more information on Renoir, see no. 54.

In 2012 the Cook Islands chose *The Sleeping Bather* to represent the artist Pierre-August Renoir. Though not his most famous painting, it was one of his best nudes.

COLLECTING DIFFICULTY

Easy. The Sleeping Bather coins are easy to locate online, but they typically run close to $300 or $400 each.

***Seated Bather*, by Renoir, 1903.**

No. 95

SOLOMIYA KRUSHELNYTSKA

Fortunately, recording technology was far enough along during Solomiya's life that some of her performances can still be heard today. Several of her 1902, 1906, 1912, and 1928 performances can be heard by searching under her name at youtube.com.

Solomiya in a fancy gown.

Solomiya Krushelnytska was a world-famous operatic soprano who sang from the early 1890s until the late 1920s. She was well known in European circles, but she was (and is) relatively unknown in America.

The author could find no biography in English of Solomiya's life, so the following is built from several different sources on the Internet. First, there is the spelling of her name. Solomiya Krushelnytska seems to be the favored Anglicized version, but others include Salomea Krusceniski and Solomeja Kruszhelnicka. On the cabinet cards she handed out to fans, she spelled her name Kruszelnicka. She was born in 1872 or 1873 in Lviv or Bliavyntsi in present-day Ukraine. She studied music at the Lviv Conservatory from 1891 to 1893, after which she began singing professionally. Her first appearances were in Poland and Russia; later, she performed in Italy, Spain, Portugal, and South America (another source claims she performed in America, as well). She is credited with saving Giacomo Puccini's "Madame Butterfly," which opened in 1904 in Milan, Italy, to a poor reception. After revising the production and adding Solomiya in the lead role, Puccini achieved the success he envisioned.

In 1920 Solomiya left the opera in favor of becoming a touring concert singer, where much of her focus was on Ukrainian folk songs and composers. She died in 1952.

Solomiya appears on the obverse of a 1997 Ukrainian 2-hryvnia coin with her name above (knowledge of the Cyrcillic alphabet and the Russian language is required to make any sense of the legend); her life and death dates appear below. She is shown in profile wearing an ornate costume and an oversized hat with what appear to be ostrich feathers.

The elegant Solomiya Krushelnytska appears on the front of this Ukrainian 2 hryvnia of 1997. Note the Cyrillic spelling of her name above her head.

COLLECTING DIFFICULTY

Easy. A quick search revealed several online offerings of the 1997 Ukrainian Solomiya coin; they were all priced above $100.

Anne Bonny was a notorious female pirate who ravaged the Caribbean Sea in the early 18th century with her lover "Calico Jack" Rackham, captain of the *Revenge*. Also aboard, disguised as a man, was Mary Read, another famous piratess whose story is just as fantastic as Anne's. We learn of them from Captain Charles Johnson's *A General History of the Robberies and Murders of the Most Notorious Pyrates*, published in 1724. Actually, the true author of the book is believed to be Daniel Dafoe, known famously for *Robinson Crusoe*; if this is so, many of the stories of Anne and Mary are probably nothing more than fiction. Nonetheless, they are fascinating stories that have been repeated so many times that they are presented as fact.

Anne Bonny was born in March 1702 as the daughter of William Cormac, a lawyer, and his maid, Peg Brennan, with whom he had been having an illicit affair (Johnson/Dafoe spun an interesting yarn using silver spoons to explain how the affair was uncovered). Following difficulties in Ireland, William, Peg, and Anne sailed for the New World and ended up in the Bahamas. When Anne was 13, Peg died, and Anne took over as mistress of the household. She reportedly attacked or killed another girl with a knife in a fit of her infamous temper. At 16 she met, fell in love with, and married James Bonny, a suspected pirate. James accepted the British government's offer of clemency and became an informant for the Crown. Anne became pregnant but at the same time became embroiled with Calico Jack. She gave birth to a son, left him with James Bonny, and joined Calico Jack on his pirate ship. There are many more details to the story, but one of the most significant is that Anne became attracted to one of the sailors on the *Revenge*—that sailor turned out to be the pirate Mary Read in a man's disguise. Ultimately, Anne, Mary, and Calico Jack were captured, but only Anne escaped execution.

Anne Bonny appears on the obverse of a colorized 1995 Cuban peso. She is shown in pirate regalia, her shirt opened, brandishing a cutlass in her right hand. Tall-masted ships appear in the background. Private firms have painted over Queen Elizabeth's portrait on 2010 East Caribbean States 25-cent pieces with additional images of Anne (and other pirates), but these appear to be novelties made for collectors, rather than official issues.

No doubt is left in the viewer's mind that Anne Bonny was a female pirate. American collectors are not allowed to import—yet—this colorized Cuban peso of 1995.

COLLECTING DIFFICULTY

Difficult. America (and eBay) prohibit the trading of coins from Cuba. However, this may change because the U.S. government, in late 2014, moved to restore diplomatic relations with Cuba. As of this writing, the embargo against Cuban coins continues.

No. 96

ANNE BONNY

Anne Bonny disguised herself as a boy when she was young; Mary Read disguised herself as a man nearly her entire life.

An engraving of Anne Bonny by Benjamin Cole, 1724.

No. 97

ELENA ALADOVA

The National Art Museum is located in the capital city of Minsk. Belarus, a former member of the Soviet Union, is a small country bordered by Russia, Ukraine, Poland, Lithuania, and Latvia.

Elena Aladova worked for the National Museum of Belarus for 33 years, becoming the Director of the Gallery and receiving the title of Honored Art Worker of the BSSR.

Elena Aladova is a relatively unknown figure, at least to American eyes and ears, but in the country of Belarus she is a revered figure in the art world. She is credited with the rebuilding of the art collection of the State Art Gallery (now the National Art Museum of the Republic of Belarus) after the Nazis looted and plundered the museum in World War II.

As late as 1941, the State Art Gallery contained more than 2,700 works, including religious artwork, a collection of Slutsk sashes, French tapestries, furniture, porcelain, handmade woolen bedspreads, and Russian paintings. Unfortunately, a catalog of the collection was not completed before the arrival of the Nazi occupiers, nor did the Nazi inventory of the collection survive. Portions of the collection went to Germany and other pieces simply disappeared. In 1944 museum staff attempted to reconstruct an inventory of the collection from memory, but this was merely an academic exercise, because only a small portion of the collection was ever recovered. Elena was instrumental in rebuilding the collection with recovered artwork and the addition of works gathered from other countries and museums. By 1946 the collection had grown to more than 300 works, necessitating a larger display area. Aladova worked with architect Mikhail Baklanov to create the building now known as the National Art Museum. By the time of the museum's dedication in 1957, the collection had already grown to the size of the prewar inventory.

In 2007 the museum held an exhibition to commemorate the 100th anniversary of Elena's birth and her important contributions.

Belarus commissioned the Mint of Poland to strike a special commemorative silver coin in 2007 featuring a portrait of Elena on the reverse, her hand on her chin, standing in front of a decorative frame. Her name and life dates appear in the left field along with a facsimile of her signature. The obverse of the coin shows the arms of the Republic of Belarus above a representation of the National Art Museum of Belarus, which houses the collection rebuilt by Elena.

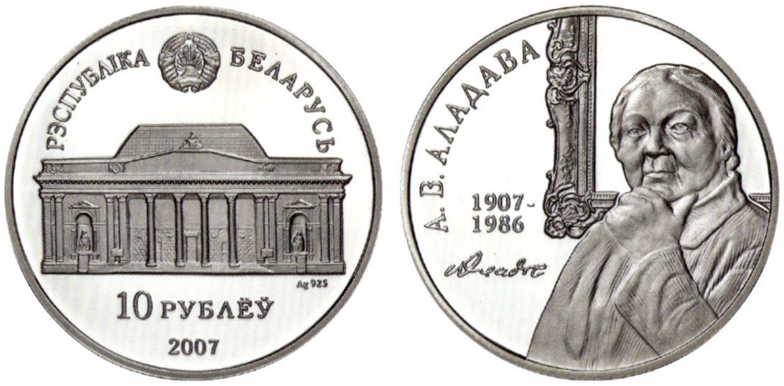

The great Belarussian art historian, Elena Aladova, as she appears on the reverse of a silver coin commemorating the 100th anniversary of her birth.

COLLECTING DIFFICULTY

Easy. The 2007 Belarus rouble coin has a small mintage of only 4,000 pieces, but it is affordable and can be found with relative ease online for less than $50.

No. 98

EUNICE KENNEDY SHRIVER

Eunice Kennedy Shriver is credited with founding the Special Olympics in 1968, giving children with intellectual disabilities the opportunity to participate in physical activities and compete in athletic competitions. The Special Olympics was an outgrowth of a day-camp Eunice started in 1962 known as Camp Shriver. Approximately 1,500 children participated in the 1968 event; in 2014 her son Timothy Shriver, the current chairman of the Special Olympics, noted that more than 180 countries hold Special Olympic games in which more than four million athletes compete.

Eunice was born Eunice Mary Kennedy in July 1921, the daughter of Joseph P. and Rose Fitzgerald Kennedy. Her brothers included future president John F. Kennedy, future U.S. attorney general Robert Kennedy, and future U.S. senator Theodore "Ted" Kennedy. She graduated from Stanford University in 1943 with a Bachelor of Science degree in sociology, laying the foundation for her later work with children with intellectual disabilities. In 1953 she married Sargent Shriver, who later became a U.S. ambassador to France. The couple had five children including Maria Shriver, who later married Arnold Schwarzenegger.

Eunice's tireless efforts to advocate for children with intellectual disabilities led to numerous awards, including the Presidential Medal of Freedom (presented by Ronald Reagan in 1984), a papal knighthood from Pope Benedict XVI (Eunice was a Roman Catholic), and many others.

Eunice died at the age of 88 on August 10, 2009, two weeks before her brother Ted.

In 1995 the United States issued a Special Olympics World Games silver dollar featuring a profile bust of Eunice Shriver facing right. The reverse of the coin features a rose, a Special Olympics award medal, and her quote "As we hope for the best in them, hope is reborn in us."

This 1995 U.S. silver dollar promoted the Special Olympics and its founder, Eunice Shriver. A portion of the proceeds from the sale of this coin benefitted the Special Olympics.

COLLECTING DIFFICULTY

Easy. The Eunice Shriver / Special Olympics silver dollar is readily available and affordable in both Uncirculated and Proof formats. The value in either case is about $40.

Eunice Shriver was the first living woman to appear on a U.S. coin and one of only five people in the history of American numismatics to have been accorded that honor.

The International Olympic Committee is fiercely protective of their name and symbols, but in 1971 they sanctioned the use of the word "Olympics" by the Special Olympics.

Eunice Kennedy Shriver was awarded the Presidential Medal of Freedom in 1984 for her work on behalf of those with intellectual disabilities.

No. 99

LOU HOOVER

The Lou Hoover house in Palo Alto, California, is now the residence of the president of Stanford University. Herbert Hoover proposed to Lou via telegraph, and she accepted via the same method. The Hoovers often conversed in Chinese to keep their conversations private from American ears. Lou had a large gap between her front teeth, which is why she never smiled in photographs.

In 1894, Lou Hoover enrolled at Stanford University as the only female geology major.

Lou Henry Hoover is one of the lesser-known American First Ladies. Nonetheless, like all the 100 Greatest Women on Coins, she has a great story to tell.

Lou was born in 1874 in Waterloo, Iowa, the daughter of Charles Henry and Florence Weed. As a young girl, she enjoyed camping, hunting, riding horses, taxidermy, and geology. In 1894 she became the first female geology student at Stanford University. While at Stanford, Lou met a young man named Herbert Hoover, a mining engineer who shared many of the same interests. They married after Lou's graduation and eventually moved to China, where Lou accompanied her husband on his extensive travels throughout the country. She became fluent in Chinese and remains the only First Lady to claim that skill.

Prior to becoming First Lady, Lou was active in the war-relief efforts led by her husband in Belgium from 1914 to 1917. She was active in the Girl Scouts, serving as president of the organization from 1922 to 1925. As First Lady, Lou combined the normal social duties of the president's wife with a decidedly activist agenda. She angered Southerners when she invited Jessie De Priest, the black wife of black congressman Oscar De Priest, to a White House tea party. She participated in relief efforts during the Great Depression and pushed the Girl Scouts to implement relief programs.

In 2014 the U.S. Mint struck a gold $10 First Spouse coin and a related bronze First Spouse medal honoring Lou as the wife of the 31st president. The $10 gold coin bears a portrait of Lou on the obverse, her head turned three-quarters to the viewer's right. The reverse shows a radio of the type Americans used in 1929 to receive the first public address ever made by a First Lady. The bronze First Spouse medal is nearly identical but is free of the slogans and legends required on the gold coin.

Lou Hoover as she appears on her First Spouse coin. She was the first presidential wife to deliver a public address over the radio.

COLLECTING DIFFICULTY

Easy. Both the gold First Spouse coin and its related bronze medal are easily located, though the former can be expensive because it contains half an ounce of .9999 pure gold.

Vesta was the Roman goddess of the hearth and home (in Greek mythology she was known as Hestia). In the daily lives of the Romans, Vesta was among the most important deities, for she was revered not only in the home but in the public sphere as well. A state-supported cult, the Vestal Virgins, grew up around her. The Vestal Virgins were an elite group of women, usually no more than six at a time, who were selected at a young age and sworn to celibacy for 30 years. Their primary function as priestesses was to keep the sacred fire in Vesta's temple lit continuously so that Roman citizens had uninterrupted access to fire for their homes. The Vestals were among the most privileged women in all of Rome. When they walked through the streets, an attendant led the way. They were given privileged seating at games and theatrical performances. When the Vestals retired from service, they were given a dowry and allowed to marry.

The Vestal order lasted for nearly 1,000 years and ended in 394 AD, when Emperor Theodosius I extinguished the sacred fire for the last time.

Vesta is a common theme on ancient Roman coins beginning circa 60 BC and running until approximately 270 AD. Vesta can be seen on the reverses of coins issued for Caligula, Julia Mamea, Lucilla Augusta, Cornelia Supera, Nero, Julia Domna (no. 49 among the 100 Greatest Women on Coins), and others. She is shown most often in a standing position holding the Palladium or seated left on a throne. Less frequently, she is shown standing in a temple with her name in the field above.

The goddess Vesta appears on the front of this ancient Roman silver denarius of L. Cassius Longinus from approximately 60 BC.

COLLECTING DIFFICULTY

Easy. Ancient Roman coins with depictions of Vesta are very common, and they come in a wide variety of types. Prices start at around $150 and go up quickly based on condition and rarity.

No. 100

VESTA (HESTIA)

The Palladium was a wooden statue made in the image of Pallas, the daughter of Triton, who was raised along with Athena (see no. 27). While practicing martial arts one day, Athena accidentally killed Pallas. In her grief, Athena constructed the statue, which was thrown from the heavens and eventually ended up at Troy, where it provided certain safety for the city.

Any Vestal Virgin that violated her oath of celibacy was subject to being buried alive, so one can understand the controversy when Emperor Elagabalus married a Vestal Virgin in 220 AD.

An engraving of Vesta by Wenceslaus Hollar.

This book is dedicated to my wife, Maggie, the greatest woman in my world.

Writing this book has been one of the most enjoyable experiences of my career. Much of that enjoyment has come from the interactions with the people who helped along the way. This book would not be in your hands without their expertise, wisdom, support, and encouragement. I offer my sincerest gratitude and thanks to the following (in random order):

Margaret, my wife, with whom I will have shared 36 years of marriage as this book debuts. Thank you for your love, patience, and forbearance, and for creating a world that now includes three children and three grandchildren.

Phil Arnold, photographer extraordinaire at the Professional Coin Grading Service, whose numismatic images are among the best in the world.

Barbara Talbot, my mother, and **Chrystel Rosenthal**, my sister, for valuable editorial comments.

Todd Pollock, another of the great numismatic photographers, who really helped me out in a bind.

Charmy Harker, aka "The Penny Lady," one of the most visible women in numismatics today. She was the first to hear the pitch for this book and helped get support from the Women in Numismatics organization.

All the individuals, numismatic firms, and auction houses that provided images.

Women in Numismatics (WIN), for the fine work they do in promoting numismatics to and for women. WIN supports two groups of women: those who are already active in numismatics as dealers, spouses, staff, and collectors; and the women who should be in numismatics. They help get the word out that there is no "silver ceiling" in our hobby. The leadership of WIN embraced this project and opened the voting to all their members, thus making the rankings as objective as a subjective voting process could be.

The WIN members whose votes determined the final rankings (in alphabetical order): Carrie Best, Sherry Briggs, Kari Brower, Beth Deisher, Kathy Freeland, Robin Grace, Charmy Harker, Nancy Kelly, Suzanne Kern, Mary Lannin, Myrna Lighterman, James Motley, Walt Ostromecki, Bonnie Sabel, Kathy Skelton, Laura Tomaszek, Debbie Williams, and John and Nancy Wilson.

Don Willis, president of the Professional Coin Grading Service (PCGS), whose expansion of PCGS into Europe and China makes it easier to find certified coins with images of women.

David Hall, president of Collectors Universe and founder of PCGS, a mentor and visionary in the numismatic world.

Jeff Garrett, the author of the first numismatic 100 Greatest™ book, a good friend, and a great writer with whom I have coauthored several books.

The management and editors at **Whitman Publishing**, for giving the green-light and enthusiastic support to this project, and for polishing my work into the book you hold in your hands.

All the women in this book whose lives and stories have changed the world.

Ron Guth is a recognized authority on United States and German coins. He is a licensed Certified Public Accountant who has been involved professionally in numismatics for nearly 40 years as a collector, dealer, researcher, and writer. His books and articles have earned numerous awards, including the American Numismatic Association's Heath Literary and Olga & Wayte Raymond awards, the Numismatic Literary Guild's Best Numismatic Investment Book and Book of the Year awards, and the Professional Numismatic Guild's Best Book of the Year award. In 2003 Ron received the prestigious President's Award from the American Numismatic Association in recognition of his numerous contributions to numismatics. In 2014 Ron was named the American Numismatic Association's Numismatist of the Year.

Ron created the CoinFacts Web site (now PCGS CoinFacts) in 1999 and currently heads the PCGS CoinFacts division at Collectors Universe. He has served in various capacities at Collectors Universe since 2004, including as Director of Numismatic Research and President of the Professional Coin Grading Service.

Ron and his wife Maggie have been married for more than 36 years and have three children and three granddaughters. They live close to the ocean in San Diego, California, where they enjoy sailing, rowing, biking, cooking, and being grandparents.

Other Books by Ron Guth

2001—*Coin Collecting For Dummies*, first edition
2002—*United States Proof and Mint Sets 1936–2002* (with Bill Gale)
2003—*100 Greatest U.S. Coins*, first edition (with Jeff Garrett)
2005—*United States Coinage: A Study by Type* (with Jeff Garrett)
2005—*100 Greatest U.S. Coins*, second edition (with Jeff Garrett)
2006—*Encyclopedia of U.S. Gold Coins 1795–1933*, first edition (with Jeff Garrett)
2008—*Encyclopedia of U.S. Gold Coins 1795–1933*, second edition (with Jeff Garrett)
2008—*Coin Collecting for Dummies*, second edition (with Neil S. Berman)
2008—*100 Greatest U.S. Coins*, third edition (with Jeff Garrett)
2010—*Auction Prices Realized for PCGS-graded German Coins*, first edition
2011—*Auction Prices Realized for PCGS-graded German Coins*, second edition
2012—*Auction Prices Realized for Certified German Coins*, first edition
2013—*Auction Prices Realized for Certified German Coins*, second edition

Image Credits

The image of Mother Teresa on page 7 was provided by **Catwalker**. The portrait of Susan B. Anthony on page 11 was provided by **Everett Historical**. The image of Princess Diana on page 13 is courtesy of **Irisphoto1**. The painting of Martha Washington (page 16) was provided by the **White House Website** (www.whitehouse.gov). The photograph of Queen Elizabeth II at the Goddard Space Flight Center (page 23) is courtesy of the **National Aeronautics and Space Administration** (NASA). The **White House Historical Association** provided the portrait of Dolley Madison (page 27). The coin image of Florence Nightingale (page 28) is courtesy of **Fritz Rudolf Kunker (GMBH)**. The image of the Statue of Liberty (page 31) was provided by **Alfredo Cerra**. **Gerhard Hirsch Nachfolger** provided the coin image for Grace Kelly on page 33. The photograph of the statue of Nike (page 34) was provided by **Henner Damke**. The photograph of the female athlete (page 37) is courtesy of **BikeRiderLondon**. *Brontë Sisters* on page 40 is a digital restoration of the original courtesy of **Dcoetzee**. Visual artist **Barry Brown Jr.** of Fort Worth, Texas, created the portraits for Cleopatra Thea (page 41) and Julia Maesa (page 92). Coin images of Mother Earth (page 44) and Athena-Nike (page 91) are courtesy of **Numismatica Ars Classica**, London. **Wellcome Images**, London, provided images of Eve (page 50) and the breastfeeding mother (page 77). The coin image for Marie Antoinette (page 51) was provided by the **Austrian Mint (Münze Österreich)**. eBay seller **Invercoin** provided the coin image for Hatshepsut on page 52. The photograph of Victory (page 54) is courtesy of **Zwiebackesser**. **Claudio Divizia** provided the photo of Boudica on page 61. **Bruun Rasmussen** of Denmark provided the coin image for Cleopatra I Syra (page 66). The two images on page 66 and 67 are from the same statue—historical evidence is inconclusive as to which queen the figure actually depicts. One of the coin images of Cleopatra Selene II (page 67) is courtesy of **Numismatik Lanz München**. The photograph of Helvetia on the Federal Palace of Switzerland in Bern (page 72) is courtesy **Andreas Praefcke**. Coin images for the Native Woman (page 74), Ingrid Bergman (page 98), *Sleeping Bather* (page 105), and Anne Bonny (page 107) are courtesy of **Todd Pollock**. **Rebecca "Rivka" Levine** contributed a photograph of herself playing her harp (page 78). **Gorny & Mosch (GMBH)** provided coin images of Audrey Hepburn (page 80) and Livia Drusilla (page 94). *The Charity of Saint Elizabeth of Hungary* (page 82) was provided by the **Art Renewal Center** of Port Reading, New Jersey. Photographs of Indira Gandhi (page 86) and Queen Juliana (page 73) are courtesy of the **National Archives of the Netherlands**. The portrait of Margaret Thatcher (page 88) was provided by the **Margaret Thatcher Foundation**, Washington, D.C. The coin image for Queen Olympias (page 89) is courtesy of **Münzkabinett Staatlichen Museen zu Berlin**. The main coin image on page 102 for the Angel is courtesy of **Bigsilvercoins.com**. The photograph of the Angel bearing Veronica's Veil (page 102) is courtesy of **Yair Haklai**. On page 105, the image of Renoir's *Seated Bather* is courtesy of the **Ibiblio Web Museum**, Paris. On page 108, the photograph of Elena Aladova is courtesy of Alla Gavrilova and the **National Art Museum of Ukraine**, Kiev. The **John F. Kennedy Presidential Library and Museum** of Boston, Massachusetts, provided the portrait of Eunice Kennedy-Shriver on page 109.

Goldberg Coins & Collectibles Inc. provided multiple coin images. **Heritage Auctions** provided multiple coin and portrait images. The **Library of Congress** provided certain historical images. The **Professional Coin Grading Service** (PCGS) provided the majority of coin images. **Stack's Bowers Galleries** provided several coin images.

"The Eunice Kennedy Shriver Story." Accessed February 22, 2105. www.eunicekennedyshriver.org/bios/eks

Airport-Data.com. Accessed December 14, 2014. www.airport-data.com/aircraft/photo/000172563L.html

Alexander, John T. *Catherine the Great: Life and Legend*. New York: Oxford University Press, 1989.

Ali, Abdullah Yusuf, trans. *The Qur'an: Translation*. Elmhurst, NY: Tahrike Tarsile Qur'an, 2009.

Allgor, Catherine. *A Perfect Union: Dolley Madison and the Creation of the American Nation*. New York: Henry Holt & Co., 2006.

Apple, Rima D. *Mothers and Medicine: A Social History of Infant Feeding, 1890–1950*. Madison, WI: University of Wisconsin Press, 1987.

Appolodorus and Robin Hard, trans. *The Library of Greek Mythology*. Oxford, England: Oxford University Press, 2008.

Baker, Jean Harvey. *Mary Todd Lincoln: A Biography*. New York: W.W. Norton & Co., 2008.

Barker, Juliet. *The Brontës: A Life In Letters*. Woodstock, NY: Overlook Press, 1998.

Barrett, Anthony A. *Livia: First Lady of Imperial Rome*. New Haven, CT: Yale University Press, 2002.

Barry, Kathleen. *Susan B. Anthony: A Biography of a Singular Feminist*. New York: New York University Press, 1988.

Barton, Simon. *A History of Spain*, second edition. Houndmills, Basingstoke, Hampshire, England: Palgrave Macmillan, 2009.

Bausum, Ann. *With Courage and Cloth: Winning the Fight for a Woman's Right to Vote*. Washington, DC: National Geographic, 2004.

Berenson, Edward. *The Statue of Liberty: A Transatlantic Story*. New Haven, CT: Yale University Press, 2012.

Bergman, Ingrid and Alan Burgess. *Ingrid Bergman: My Story*. New York: Delacorte Press, 1980.

Berkin, Carol. *Civil War Wives: The Lives & Times of Angelina Grimké Weld, Varina Howell Davis & Julia Dent Grant*. New York: Vintage Books, 2009.

Birley, Anthony. *Septimius Severus: The African Emperor*. London: Routledge, 1988.

Bradford, Sarah. *Princess Grace*. New York: Stein and Day, 1984.

Brady, Patricia. *Martha Washington: An American Life*. New York: Penguin Books, 2006.

Burdette, Roger W. *Renaissance of American Coinage: 1916–1921*. Great Falls, VA: Seneca Mill Press, 2005.

Burkett, Elinor. *Golda*. New York: Harper Perennial, 2009.

Cable, Simon. "A His and Hers Guide To Classic Screen Goddesses: Why Men Like Ursula Andress and Women Prefer Audrey Hepburn." *Daily Mail*. Accessed December 21, 2014. www.dailymail.co.uk/femail/article-1263547/Why-men-like-Ursula-Andress-women-prefer-Audrey-Hepburn.html

Campbell, John M. and Donna Campbell. *War Paint: Fighter Nose Art from WWII & Korea*. Osceola, WI: Motorbooks International, 1990.

Carney, Elizabeth Donnelly. *Arsinoë of Egypt and Macedon: A Royal Life*. New York: Oxford University Press, 2013.

Carney, Elizabeth. *Olympias: Mother of Alexander the Great*. New York: Routledge, 2006.

Carr, Raymond, ed. *Spain: A History*. Oxford, England: Oxford University Press, 2000.

Central Texas Wing Web site. www.cafcentex.com/aircraft/B25.php, accessed 1/4/2015.

Chandler, Charlotte. *Ingrid Bergman: A Personal Biography*. New York: Simon & Schuster, 2007.

Charles River Editors. *History's Famous Women Pirates: Grace O'Malley, Anne Bonny and Mary Read*. N.p.: Charles River Editors, n.d.

Church, Clive H. and Randolph C. Head. *A Concise History of Switzerland*. New York: Cambridge University Press, 2014.

Clayman, Dee L. *Berenice II and the Golden Age of Ptolemaic Egypt*. New York: Oxford University Press, 2014.

Clayton, Paul. *White Seed: The Untold Story of the Lost Colony of Roanoke*. N.p., Paul Clayton, 2009.

Colman, Penny. *Elizabeth Cady Stanton and Susan B. Anthony: A Friendship That Changed the World*. New York: Henry Holt and Co., 2011.

Cook, Blanche Wiesen. *Eleanor Roosevelt*, volume 1: 1884–1933. New York: Viking, 1992.

Cook, Blanche Wiesen. *Eleanor Roosevelt*, volume 2: 1933–1938. New York: Viking, 1999.

Cook, Sir Edward Tyas. *The Life of Florence Nightingale*, volume 1. San Bernardino, CA: Forgotten Books, 2014.

Cook, Sir Edward Tyas. *The Life of Florence Nightingale*, volume 2. San Bernardino, CA: Forgotten Books, 2014.

Cooney, Kara. *The Woman Who Would Be King: Hatshepsut's Rise to Power in Ancient Egypt*. New York: Crown, 2014.

Crankshaw, Edward. *Maria Theresa*. London: Bloomsbury Reader, 2013.

Curie, Eve and Vincent Sheean, trans. *Madame Curie: A Biography*. New York: Da Capo Press, 2001.

Curtis, Gregory. Disarmed: *The Story of the Venus de Milo*. New York: Vintage Books, 2004.

Dahmen, Karsten. "Alexander in Gold and Silver: Reassessing Third Century AD Medallions from Aboukir and Tarsos." *American Journal of Numismatics*, second series 20 (2008). pp. 493–546. www.academia.edu/357735/Alexander_in_Gold_and_Silver_Reassessing_Third_century_AD_Medallions_from_Aboukir_and_Tarsos (accessed February 4, 2015).

Defoe, Daniel and Manuel Schonhorn, ed. *A General History of the Pyrates*. Mineola, NY: Dover Publication, 1999.

Dennison, Matthew. Livia, *Empress of Rome: A Biography*. New York: St. Martin's Press, 2010.

Dodson, Aidan and Dyan Hilton. *The Complete Royal Families of Ancient Egypt*. London: Thames & Hudson, 2010.

Eddy, Samuel. "The Gold in the Athena Parthenos." *American Journal of Archaeology*, volume 81, number 1 (Winter, 1977), pp. 107–111. www.jstor.org/stable/503656?saveCitation=true&confirm=add&seq=1#page_scan_tab_contents (accessed February 2, 2015).

Edmonds III, Radcliffe G. *Myths of the Underworld Journey: Plato, Aristophanes, and the "Orphic" Gold Tablets*. Cambridge: Cambridge University Press, 2004.

Ellis, Joseph J. *First Family: Abigail and John Adams*. New York: Alfred A. Knopf, 2010.

Esdaile, Charles J. *Spain in the Liberal Age: From Constitution to Civil War, 1808–1939*. Oxford, England: Blackwell Publishers, 2000.

Feist, Peter H. *Pierre-Auguste Renoir, 1841–1919: A Dream Of Harmony*. New York: Barnes & Noble Books, 2000.

Ferrer, Sean Hepburn. *Audrey Hepburn, An Elegant Spirit*. New York: Atria Books, 2003.

Finneran, Richard J., ed. *The Collected Poems of W.B. Yeats*. New York: Scribner Paperback Poetry, 1996.

Flanagan, Sabina. *Hildegard of Bingen, 1089–1179: A Visonary Life*. New York: Routledge, 1998.

Foley, Helene P. *The Homeric Hymn to Demeter: Translation, Commentary, and Interpretative Essays*. Princeton, NJ: Princeton University Press, 1994.

Fox, Matthew. *Illuminations of Hildegard of Bingen*. Rochester, VT: Bear & Company, 2002.

Fraser, Nicholas and Marysa Navarro. *Evita: The Real Life of Eva Perón*. New York: W.W. Norton & Co., 1980.

Gauguin, Paul and O.F. Theis, trans. *Noa, Noa: The Tahitian Journal*. New York: Dover Publications, 1985.

Hamann, Brigitte. Sissi: *Elisabeth, Empress of Austria*. New York: Taschen, 1997.

Haugen, Brenda. *Martha Washington: First Lady of the United States*. Minneapolis: Compass Point Books, 2005.

Herrmann, Dorothy. *Helen Keller: A Life*. Chicago: University of Chicago Press, 2007.

Hesiod, Theognis, and Dorothea Wender, trans. *Theogony, Works and Days, and Elegies*. New York: Penguin Books, 1973.

Hingley, Richard, and Christina Unwin. *Boudica: Iron Age Warrior Queen*. London: Hambledon Continuum, 2005.

Hoffman, William. *Queen Juliana: The Story of the Richest Woman in the World*. New York: Harcourt, Brace, Jovanovich, 1979.

Holton, Woody. *Abigail Adams*. New York: Free Press, 2010.

Holum, Kenneth G. *Theodosian Empresses: Women and Imperial Dominion in Late Antiquity*. Berkeley, CA: University of California Press,

Hopkins, Andrea. *The Book of Guinevere: Legendary Queen of Camelot*. Glasgow, Scotland: Saraband, 2004.

Howe, Marvin. "Teresa de Francisci, Miss Liberty Model for Coin, Dies at 92." *The New York Times* Web site, October 22, 1990, www.nytimes.com/1990/10/22/obituaries/teresa-de-francisci-miss-liberty-model-for-coin-dies-at-92.html, accessed January 6, 2015.

Hudson, Marjorie. *Searching for Virginia Dare: On The Trail of the Lost Colony of Roanoke Island*. Winston-Salem, NC: Press 53, 2013.

Hupka, Robert. *Michelangelo: Pietà*. New York: Crown Publishers, 1984.

Hutchins, Chris and Thompson, Peter. *Diana's Nightmare: The Family*. N.p.: Christopher Hutchins, Ltd., 2014.

Hux, Clete. "Angelmania." Watchman Fellowship. Accessed February 10, 2015. www.watchman.org/articles/new-age/angelmania/.

Jones, Cecilia Anne. *The Life of S. Elizabeth of Hungary, Duchess of Thuringia*. N.p.: Elibron Classics, 2005.

Jones, Christopher P., ed. *Philostratus, The Life of Apollonius of Tyana*, books 1–4. Cambridge, MA: Harvard University Press, 2005.

Jones, Christopher P., ed. *Philostratus, The Life of Apollonius of Tyana*, books 5–8. Cambridge, MA: Harvard University Press, 2005.

Kann, Robert A. *A History of the Habsburg Empire, 1526–1918*. Berkeley, CA: University of California Press, 1980.

Keller, Helen. *The Story of My Life*. Mineola, NY: Dover Publications, 1996.

Keller, Helen. *The World I Live In: A Collection of Essays*. Mineloa, NY: Dover Publications, 2009.

King, Greg. *The Last Empress: The Life and Times of Alexandra Feodorovna, Tsarina of Russia*. New York: Citadel Press, 1996.

Kousalas, D.G. *The Life and Times of Constantine the Great: The First Christian Emperor*. N.p., D.G. Kousalas, 2007.

Lacey, Robert. *Monarch: The Life and Reign of Elizabeth II*. New York: Free Press, 2003.

Lash, Joseph P. *Eleanor and Franklin*. New York: W.W. Norton & Co., 2014.

Leaming, Barbara. *Jacqueline Bouvier Kennedy Onassis: The Untold Story*. New York: Thomas Dunne Books, 2014.

Levick, Barbara. *Julia Domna: Syrian Empress*. New York: Routledge, 2007.

Longworth, Philip. *The Three Empresses: Catherine I, Anne, and Elizabeth of Russia*. New York: Holt, Rinehart and Winston, 1972.

MacCullough, Diarmaid. *Christianity: The First Three Thousand Years*. New York: Viking, 2009.

Mathews, Nancy Mowll. *Paul Gauguin: An Erotic Life*. New Haven, CT: Yale University Press, 2001.

Meir, Golda. *My Life*. London: Cox & Wyman, 1975.

Meltzer, Milton. *Slavery: A World History*. New York: Da Capo Press, 1993.

Ménard, Michèle. *Coins of the Modern Olympic Games*, volume 1. N.p.: Michèle Ménard, 1991.

Michael Beschloss, ed. *Jacqueline Kennedy: Historic Conversations on Life With John F. Kennedy, Interviews With Arthur M. Schlesinger, Jr.*, 1964. New York: Hyperion, 2011.

Miller, Lee. *Roanoke: Solving the Mystery of the Lost Colony*. New York: Penguin Books, 2000.

Miller, Marla R. *Betsy Ross and the Making of America*. New York: Henry Holt & Co., 2010.

Mitchell, Elizabeth. *Liberty's Torch: The Great Adventure to Build the Statue of Liberty*. New York: Atlantic Monthly Press, 2014.

Monaghan, Patricia. *The New Book of Goddesses & Heroines*. St. Paul, MN: Llewellyn Publications, 2000.

Mother Teresa. *In the Heart of the World: Thoughts, Stories, and Prayers*. Novato, CA: New World Library, 2010.

National Park Service. "Black Statue of Liberty—Summary Report." Accessed December 20, 2014. www.nps.gov/stli/historyculture/black-statue-of-liberty.htm

New Advent. "Sts. Faith, Hope & Charity." Accessed February 9, 2015. www.newadvent.org/cathen/05766a.htm

New York Times. "Criticises Museum Sculpture Settings." May 21,1920. Accessed December 28, 2014. query.nytimes.com/gst/abstract.html?res=9D02E1DE103FE432A25752C2A9639C946195D6CF

O'Laughlin, Michael C. *The Irish Book of Arms: Genealogy & Heraldry*. Kansas City, MO: Irish Genealogical Foundation, 2000.

Orthodoz Church in America. "Martyr Sophia and her three daughters at Rome." Accessed February 9, 2015. oca.org/saints/lives/1999/09/17/102638-martyr-sophia-and-her-three-daughters-at-rome

Ovid and A.D. Melville, trans. *Metamorphoses*. New York: Oxford University Press, 1986.

Partner, Peter. *Christianity: The First Two Thousand Years*. N.p.: Seven Oaks, 1999.

Pausanias and W.H.S. Jones, trans. *Description of Greece*, books 1 and 2. Cambridge, MA: Harvard University Press, 1998.

Perón, Evita. *Evita: In My Own Words*. New York: The New Press, 1996.

Plutarch and John Dryden, trans. *The Life of Alexander the Great*. New York: Modern Library.

Pomeroy, Sarah. *Goddesses, Whores, Wives, and Slaves: Women in Classical Antiquity*. New York: Schocken Books, 1995.

Quinn, Susan. *Marie Curie: A Life*. Reading, MA: Addison-Wesley Publishing Company, 1995.

Reef, Catherine. *The Brontë Sisters: The Brief Lives of Charlotte, Emily, and Anne*. New York: Clarion Books, 2012.

Reuters. "New Anne of Green Gables Book Stirs Debate." Accessed December 19, 2014. www.reuters.com/article/2008/03/19/us-book-anne-idUSN1754861220080319

Roberts, Cokie. *Ladies of Liberty: The Women Who Shaped Our Nation*. New York: Harper Perennial, 2008.

Ronda, James P. *Lewis & Clark Among the Indians*. Lincoln, NE: University of Nebraska Press, 1998.

Roosevelt, Eleanor. *The Autobiography of Eleanor Roosevelt*. New York: Harper Perennial, 1961.

Saint Hildegard and Mark Atherton, trans. *Selected Writings: Hildegard of Bingen*. London: Penguin Books, 2001.

Saperstein, Marc. *Your Voice Like a Ram's Horn: Themes and Texts in Traditional Jewish Preaching*. Cincinnati: Hebrew Union College Press, 1996.

Sherr, Lynn. *Failure Is Impossible: Susan B. Anthony in Her Own Words*. N.p.: Times Books, 1995.

Shriver, Ted. "Special Olympics." *Ability Magazine*. Accessed February 22, 2015. abilitymagazine.com/Special-Olympics-Shriver.html

Sidey, Hugh, Jon Goodman, and Letitia Baldrige (2006). *The Kennedy Mystique: Creating Camelot: Essays*. Washington, DC: National Geographic, 2006.

Simon, John Y., ed. *The Personal Memoirs of Julia Dent Grant (Mrs. Ulysses S. Grant)*. Carbondale, IL: Southern Illinois University Press, 1975.

Spada, James. *Grace Kelly: The Secret Lives of a Princess*. New York: Doubleday, 1987.

Spenser, Edmund and P.C. Bayley, ed. *The Faerie Queene*, book 1. Oxford, England: Oxford University Press, 1966.

Spink, Kathryn. *Mother Teresa: An Authorized Biography*. New York: HarperOne, 2011.

Spoto, Donald. *Notorius: The Life of Ingrid Bergman*. New York: Harper Collins Publishers, 1997.

Spyri, Johanna. *Collection Novels*. San Bernardino, CA, 2015.

St. Aubyn, Giles. *Queen Victoria: A Portrait*. New York: Atheneum, 1992.

St. Austell, Edmund. "Salomea Krusceniski [Соломія Крушельницька]." greatoperasingers.blogspot.com/2010/08/salomea-krusceniski.html (accessed February 9, 2015).

Steinberg, Blema S. *Women in Power: The Personalities and Leadership Styles of Indira Gandhi, Golda Meir, and Margaret Thatcher*. Montreal, Canada: McGill-Queen's University Press, 2008.

Stephenson, Paul. *Constantine: Roman Emperor, Christian Victor*. New York: Overlook Press, 2010.

Summers, Anthony. *Goddess: The Secret Lives of Marilyn Monroe*. New York: Open Road, 1985.

Taraborrelli, J. Randy. *Once Upon a Time: Behind the Fairy Tale of Princess Grace and Prince Rainier*. New York: Warner Books, 2003.

Taxay, Don. *The U.S. Mint and Coinage: An Illustrated History from 1776 to the Present*. New York: Arco Publishing, 1966.

The Journals of the Lewis and Clark Expedition. University of Nebraska at Lincoln Web site, lewisandclarkjournals.unl.edu/index.html, accessed December 20, 2014.

The Open Bible: Expanded Edition. La Habra, CA: Lockman Foundation, 1985.

Turner, Justin G. and Linda Levitt Turner. *Mary Todd Lincoln: Her Life and Letters*. New York: Alfred A. Knopf, 1972.

Tyldesley, Joyce A. Hatchepsut: *The Female Pharaoh*. New York: Penguin Books, 1998.

Tyldesley, Joyce. *Nefertiti: Egypt's Sun Queen*. New York: Viking, 1998.

Ukraine.com. "Solomiya Krushelnytska Musical Museum—The Life of a Ukrainian Opera Star." Accessed February 9, 2015. www.ukraine.com/museums/solomiya-krushelnytska-musical/

Ulrich, Anna and Helen B. Dole, trans. *Recollections of Johanna Spyri's Childhood*. New York: Thomas Y. Crowell, 1925.

Vasari, Giorgio and Julia Conway Bondanella, trans. *The Lives of the Artists*. Oxford, England: Oxford University Press, 2008.

Vovk, Justin C. *In Destiny's Hands: Five Tragic Rulers, Children of Maria Theresa*. New York: iUniverse, 2010.

Walters, Lori, ed. *Lancelot and Guinevere: A Casebook*. New York: Routledge, 2002.

Weir, Alison. *The Life of Elizabeth*. New York: Ballantine Books, 2008.

White, Barbara Ehrich. *Renoir: His Life, Art, and Letters*. New York: Harry N. Abrams Publisher, 1988.

Whitehorne, John. *Cleopatras*. New York: Routledge, 1994.

Wilson, Budge. *Before Green Gables*. New York: Berkley Books, 2008.

Winged Victory of Samothrace. Louvre Web site at www.louvre.fr/en/oeuvre-notices/winged-victory-samothrace, accessed December 22, 2014.

Woodham-Smith, Cecil B. *Queen Victoria: Her Life and Times*. New York: Alfred A. Knopf, 1972.

Worsfold, T. Cato. *The History of the Vestal Virgins of Rome*. N.p., Kessinger Legacy Reprints, n.d.

Young, Nancy Beck. *Lou Henry Hoover: Activist First Lady*. Lawrence, KS: University Press of Kansas, 2004.

This checklist includes all of the women discovered in the author's survey of world coins (ancient and modern), plus write-ins from the voters, and others found while this book was being written. The checklist is separated into four categories—Allegorical Women, Women in Artwork, Goddesses, and Real Women—and each of the categories have been sorted alphabetically. Use this checklist to record the coins you have added to your collection or to determine the women you need. Finding coins for some of these women will be a real challenge. Have fun!

Allegorical Women

❑Abundance
❑Africa
❑Alice in Wonderland
❑Allegorical figure of city
❑Allegorical Women's Rights
❑America statue
❑Anatolic girl
❑Angel
❑Ann Darrow
❑Anne of Green Gables
❑ANZAC Day Nurses
❑Artwork, Venus, by Edward B. Jones
❑Athlete (badminton player)
❑Athlete (canoer)
❑Athlete (fencer)
❑Athlete (field hockey player)
❑Athlete (figure skater)
❑Athlete (gymnast)
❑Athlete (high jumper)
❑Athlete (netball players)
❑Athlete (Olympian)
❑Athlete (pole vaulter)
❑Athlete (runner)
❑Athlete (shotputter)
❑Barbie (statue)
❑Bavaria
❑Beijing Opera
❑Black woman's head
❑Bride (and groom)
❑Britannia
❑Britannia and Marianne
❑Britannia dejected, missing Liberty Cap
❑Charity
❑Cinderella
❑Colorized Women
❑Copenhagen mermaid
❑Cosette from Les Miserables
❑Countess Cherry
❑Couple kissing
❑Crowned woman
❑Czech woman
❑Dancer (Apsara)
❑Dancer (Arabian Dance)
❑Dancer (Arirang)
❑Dancer (Balinese)
❑Dancer (Ballerina
❑Dancer (Celestial)
❑Dancer (Folk)
❑Dancer (Janggo)
❑Dancer (Katkah)
❑Dancer (Legong)
❑Dancer (Ribbon)
❑Dancer (Waltzer)
❑Dancer (Yangtze)
❑Dancer (Zamba)
❑Dancers
❑Dancers (Cambodian)
❑Dancers (Folk)
❑Dancers (Mexican)
❑Democrazia
❑Dorothy of Oz
❑Dutch maiden
❑Education (Knowledge)
❑Education (Wisdom)
❑Eternity (Aeternitas)
❑Eve (and Adam)
❑Faith, Hope, Charity, and Mother Sophia
❑Flower Fairies Series (multiples)
❑Freedom
❑Freedom and Virtue
❑Gaucho woman
❑Geisha
❑Germania
❑Girl and boy holding a flag
❑Girl with rag doll
❑Goddess Securitas (Security)
❑Heidi (by Johanna Spyri)
❑Helvetia
❑Helvetia (and Lion)
❑Hope, Peace, Art, and Labor
❑International Year of the Woman
❑Italia
❑Jamila
❑Japanese woman
❑Justice
❑Kneeling nude
❑Kumgang Fairy
❑Lady with clapperboard
❑Laotian maiden
❑Liberty
❑Liberty and Britannia
❑Liberty and Justice
❑Liberty (partial nude)
❑Liberty seated
❑Liberty unchained
❑Little Red Riding Hood
❑Maiden
❑Malvina, The Fairy with the Turquoise Hair
❑Medusa
❑Merchant woman
❑Mermaid
❑Military women
❑Mirror of Galadriel
❑Miss Canada
❑Miss Liberty
❑Mother
❑Mother and child
❑Mother Russia
❑Mucha Zodiac series
❑Muse with mask and lyre
❑Nana (Émile Zola)
❑Notre Dame du Saguenay
❑Nude woman
❑Nude women
❑Nuremburg
❑Nurse with patient
❑Olympic
❑Opera role
❑Padaung woman
❑Patience
❑Peace
❑Piety and Justice
❑Pixie
❑Poetess of Song Dynasty
❑Princess Leia
❑Prussia
❑Psyche
❑Queen Amidala
❑Queen Guinevere
❑Queen of Spades
❑Radish
❑Revolution
❑Romania
❑Ruslan and Ludmilla, by Alexander Pushkin
❑Scarlett O'Hara
❑Schoolgirl (and boy)
❑Seated Liberty
❑Snow Queen
❑Snow White
❑Statue of Liberty
❑Stylized woman
❑Swaziland woman
❑The Tale of the Dead Princess and the Seven Knights, by Alexander Pushkin
❑Titanic Memorial Statue
❑Tunisian girl
❑Una
❑Veiled woman
❑Venus (nude)
❑Virgo
❑Volgograd Monument
❑White Witch
❑Wilma Flinstone and Betty Rubble
❑Winged Liberty
❑Winged Victory
❑Woman and baby
❑Woman and child
❑Woman and cow
❑Woman breastfeeding
❑Woman figure
❑Woman figures
❑Woman floating
❑Woman guerilla
❑Woman head
❑Woman holding flowers
❑Woman in outdoor market
❑Woman lute player
❑Woman matmaker
❑Woman of Wachau
❑Woman on railroad platform
❑Woman opera character
❑Woman Oueme (nude)
❑Woman paraders
❑Woman pirates
❑Woman planting oak tree
❑Woman playing pipes
❑Woman representatives of the Nile
❑Woman seated
❑Woman seated with child
❑Woman slave
❑Woman Somba (nude)
❑Woman standing
❑Woman standing at easel
❑Woman striding left
❑Woman Tae Kwan Do
❑Woman Venice
❑Woman warriors
❑Woman weaver
❑Woman weaving on board
❑Woman with conch
❑Woman with lyre
❑Woman with trident
❑Woman worker
❑Woman worker (farm wife)
❑Woman worker (planting)
❑Woman worker (silk spinner)
❑Woman worker (silk worker)
❑Women seated and standing
❑Women shouting (The Maiden's Cave)
❑Women's decade
❑Young woman writing
❑Yunona and Avos

Women in Artwork

❑*Adele Bloch-Bauer*, by Gustav Klimt
❑Annunciazone
❑Art Nouveau woman
❑*Autumn Bouquet*, by Ilya Repin
❑*Baby Girl*, by Anne Geddes
❑*Birth of Venus*, by Botticelli
❑*Briefing Time* (WWII plane nose art)
❑Carl Brullov art
❑*Clothed and Nude Maya*, by da Goya
❑Dame Edna Everage
❑*Die Erwartung*, by Gustav Klimt
❑Diego Velazquez art
❑Dürer painting
❑Expressionist woman
❑*Girl at the Window*, by Salvador Dalí
❑*Girl With A Pearl Earring*, by Vermeer
❑*Girls at the Piano*, by Auguste Renoir
❑*Insect Cage*, by Utamaro Kitagawa
❑*Judith II*, by Gustav Klimt
❑Katherina icon
❑La Pietà
❑*La Primavera*, by Botticelli
❑*La Velata*, by Raphael
❑*Lacemaker*, by Tropinin
❑*Lady With An Ermine*, by Da Vinci
❑*Leda and the Swan*, by Rubens
❑*L'Infante Marie-Marguerite*, by Diego Velazquez
❑*Margaret Olley*, by Sir William Dobell
❑Mary, mother of Jesus
❑Maternidad sculpture
❑*Memphis Belle* (WWII nose art)
❑*Mona Lisa*, by DaVinci
❑Mucha art
❑*Native Woman*, by Paul Gauguin

❑ *Nude Maya*, by Goya
❑ Paleolithic Venue
❑ *Portrait of a Young Woman*, by Raphael
❑ *Portrait of Jeanne Samary*, by Auguste Renoir
❑ *Providentia Fountain*, by Raphael Donner
❑ *Seated Woman with a Harp*, by Ivan Mestrovic
❑ *Sleeping Bather*, by Renoir
❑ St. Teresa
❑ Strobl Monument
❑ Tcho-ee-put-o-kaw
❑ The Drover's Wife
❑ *The Little Dancer*, by Degas
❑ *The Marriage of the Virgin*, by Raphael
❑ Ukraine woman
❑ Venus de Milo
❑ *Virgin of the Rocks*, by Leonardo da Vinci
❑ *Virgo*, by Kagaya
❑ Woman Crying
❑ Woman mosaic at Aquileia
❑ *Woman with Basket*, by Ivan Khrutsky
❑ *Woman with Umbrella*, by Claude Monet
❑ *Yellow Rose* (WWII plane nose art)

Goddesses

❑ Goddess
❑ Goddess (winged)
❑ Alexandria
❑ Anahit
❑ Annia Perenna
❑ Arethusa
❑ Astghik
❑ Athena (or Minerva)
❑ Athena and Nike
❑ Augusta
❑ Bast
❑ Concordia
❑ Cybele
❑ Demeter (or Ceres)
❑ Diana
❑ Europa
❑ Fame
❑ Fides
❑ Fortuna
❑ Fortuna Populi Romani
❑ Guanyin
❑ Hathor
❑ Hathor and Bat
❑ Juno
❑ Juno Sospita
❑ Kuan Yin
❑ Libertas
❑ Mazu
❑ Medusa
❑ Mercy
❑ Mother Earth
❑ Nike
❑ Nike of Warsaw
❑ Nu Wa
❑ Olympias
❑ Persephone
❑ Rape of Europa
❑ Roma
❑ Salus and Valetudo
❑ Selene
❑ Serket
❑ Vesta
❑ Victory

Real Women

❑ Abigail Adams (1744–1818)
❑ Abigail Fillmore (1798–1853)
❑ Aelia Ariadne (c. 450–525 AD)
❑ Aelia Eudocia Augusta (Athenais) (c. 401–460 AD)
❑ Aelia Eudoxia (???–404 AD)
❑ Aelia Flavia Flaccilla (???–386 AD)
❑ Aelia Galla Placidia, later Gallia Pacidia (392–450 AD)
❑ Aelia Pulcheria (c. 398–453 AD)
❑ Aelia Verina (???–484 AD)
❑ Aelia Zenonis (???–c.477 AD)
❑ Agrippina I (14 BC–33 AD)
❑ Agrippina II (16–59 AD)
❑ Aishwarya Rajya Laxmi Devi Shah (1949–2001)
❑ Alexandra Feodorovna (1872–1918)
❑ Alexandrine of Mecklenburg–Schwerin (1879–1952)
❑ Alice Paul (1885–1977)
❑ Amalie Auguste (1801–1877)
❑ Amalie of Hesse (1754–1832)
❑ Ana Katarina Zrinska (1625–1673)
❑ Anna Amalia of Brunswick–Wolfenbüttel (1739–1807)
❑ Anna Dorothea, Duchess of Saxe–Weimar (1657–1704)
❑ Anna Eleanor Roosevelt (1883–1962)
❑ Anna Harrison (1775–1864)
❑ Anna Magnani (1908–2008)
❑ Anna of Russia (1693–1740)
❑ Anna Salome of Manderscheid–Blankenheim (1628–1691)
❑ Anna Salome von Salm–Reifferscheidt
❑ Anna Sophia I (1619–1680)
❑ Anne Boleyn (1499–1536)
❑ Anne Bonny (1702–1782)
❑ Anne Elizabeth Alice Louise (1950–)
❑ Annette von Droste–Hülshoff (1797–1848)
❑ Annia Aurelia Faustina (c. 201–c. 222 AD)
❑ Annia Aurelia Galeria Lucilla (c. 148–182 AD)
❑ Annia Cupressenia Herennia Etruscilla (249–251 AD)
❑ Antonia the Younger (36 BC–37 AD)
❑ Arletty (1898–1992)
❑ Arsinoe II (316–270 BC)
❑ Audrey Hepburn (1929–1993)
❑ Augusta of Saxe–Weimar–Eisenach (1811–1890)
❑ Beatrice of Naples (1457–1508)
❑ Beatrix Wilhelmina Armgard (1938–)
❑ Berenice II (???–221 BC)
❑ Betsy Ross (1752–1836)
❑ British queens
❑ Brontë sisters
❑ Bruttia Crispina (164–191 AD)
❑ Caecilia Paulina (???–c. 236 AD)
❑ Cai Wenji (???–???)
❑ Caroline Harrison (1832–1892)
❑ Catherina–Amalia (2003–)
❑ Catherine Elizabeth "Kate" Middleton (1982–)
❑ Catherine I of Russia (1684–1727)
❑ Catherine II (the Great) of Russia (1729–1796)
❑ Celia Sanchez Mandulay (1920–1980)
❑ Charlotte Adelgonde Élise / Elisabeth Marie Wilhelmine (1896–1985)
❑ Charlotte Amalie Sophie Auguste of Sayn (1741–1803)
❑ Chris Evert (1954–)
❑ Christiane Charlotte of Württemberg–Winnental (1694–1729)
❑ Christina, Queen of Sweden (1626–1689)
❑ Christine Charlotte of Wurttemburg (1645–1699)
❑ Christine Marie of France (1606–1663)
❑ Chulabhorn Walailak (1957–)
❑ Clara Schumann (1819–1896)
❑ Clara Zetkin (1857–1933)
❑ Claudia Antonia (30–66 AD)
❑ Claudia Felicitas of Austria (1653–1676)
❑ Claudia Livilla Julia (13 BC–31 AD)
❑ Claudia Octavia (39–62 AD)
❑ Cleopatra I Syra (205–176 BC)
❑ Cleopatra Selene II (40 BC–??)
❑ Cleopatra Thea (164–121 BC)
❑ Cleopatra VII Philopator (69–30 BC)
❑ Dame Nellie Melba (1861–1931)
❑ Delilah
❑ Dessislava
❑ Didia Clara (153–??? AD)
❑ Dobrawa of Bohemia (c. 940–977)
❑ Doina Aldea–Teodorovici (1958–1992)
❑ Dolley Payne Todd Madison (1768–1849)
❑ Domitia Longina (c. 54 – c. 130 AD)
❑ Domitilla The Younger (45–66 AD)
❑ Dona Fabiola de Mora y Aragon (1928–)
❑ Dorothea Wilhelmine von Bötticher (1725–1754)
❑ Duchess of York and daughters
❑ Edith Roosevelt (1861–1948)
❑ Edith Wilson (1872–1961)
❑ Egnatia Mariniana (???–??? AD)
❑ Elena Aladova (1907–1986)
❑ Eleonora Gonzaga (1598–1655)
❑ Elisabeth Amalie Friederike (1714–1748)
❑ Elisabeth Auguste of Sulzbach (1721–1794)
❑ Elisabeth Marie of Oels (1625–1686)
❑ Eliza Johnson (1810–1876)
❑ Elizabeth "Betty" Ford (1918–2011)
❑ Elizabeth "Bess" Truman (1885–1982)
❑ Elizabeth Juliana of Schleswig–Holstein–Sønderburg–Nordborg
❑ Elizabeth MacArthur (1766–1850)
❑ Elizabeth Monroe (1768–1830)
❑ Elizabeth of Austria (1837–1898)
❑ Elizabeth of Russia (1729–1762)
❑ Elizabeth Rosemond "Liz" Taylor (1932–2011)
❑ Elizaveta Petrovna (1709–1762)
❑ Ellen Wilson (1860–1914)
❑ Emilia Plater (1806–1831)
❑ Emma of Waldeck and Pyrmont (1858–1934)
❑ Elisabeth, Empress of Austria (1837–1898)
❑ Michiko, Empress of Japan (1934–)
❑ Zewditu I, Empress of Ethiopia (1876–1930)
❑ Eunice Kennedy Shriver (1921–2009)
❑ Euphrosyne (Euphrasinta) of Polotsk (1110–1173)
❑ Evita Perón (1919–1952)
❑ Fanny Elssler (1810–1884)
❑ Faustina the Elder (c. 100–140 AD)
❑ Faustina the Younger (c. 125–175 AD)
❑ Isabella, Queen of Spain (1451-1504)
❑ Five Queens (British)
❑ Flavia Julia Constantia (c. 293–c. 330 AD)
❑ Flavia Julia Titi (64–91 AD)
❑ Flavia Maxima Fausta (289–326)
❑ Flavia Maximiana Theodora (???–??? AD)
❑ Florence Harding (1860–1924)
❑ Florence Nightingale (1820–1910)
❑ Frances Cleveland (1864–1947)
❑ Friederike Caroline Neuber (1697–1760)
❑ Fulvia (83–40 BC)
❑ Furia Sabinia Tranquillina (c. 225–after 244 AD)
❑ Gabriele Petkevicaite–Bite (1861–1943)
❑ Gabrielle Bonheur "Coco" Chanel (1883–1971)
❑ Gaia Cornelia Supera (???–??? AD)
❑ Galeria Valeria (???–315 AD)
❑ Galina Sergeyevna Ulanova (1910–1998)
❑ Georgine "Gina" Norberte Johanna Franziska Antonie Marie Raphaela von Wilczek (1921–1989)
❑ Ghena Dimitrova (1941–2005)
❑ Ginger Rogers (1911–1995)
❑ Golda Meir (1898–1978)
❑ Grace Coolidge (1879–1957)
❑ Grace Patricia Kelly (1939–1982)
❑ Greta Garbo (1905–1990)
❑ Hatshepsut (1508–1458 BC)
❑ Haydée Tamara Bunke Bider, "Tania the Guerrillera" (1937–1967)
❑ Hedwig Sophie von Brandenburg (1623–1683)
❑ Helen Keller (1880–1968)
❑ Helen Taft (1861–1943)
❑ Helena Modjeska (1840–1909)
❑ Hella Wuolijoki (1886–1954)

❑Hillary Clinton (1947–)
❑Huang Daopo (1245–1330)
❑Ida McKinley (1847–1907)
❑Ilona Zrinyi (1643–1703)
❑Imelda Marcos (1929–)
❑Indira Priyadarshini Gandhi (1917–1984)
❑Ingrid Bergman (1915–1982)
❑Irena Sendler (1910–2008)
❑Isabella Clara Eugenia of Spain (1566–1633)
❑Isabella Clara of Austria (1629–1685)
❑Isabella II of Spain (1830–1904)
❑Iulia Aquilia Severa (???–??? AD)
❑Ivana Brlić–Mažuranić (1874–1938)
❑Jacqueline Lee Bouvier Kennedy Onassis (1929–1994)
❑Jadwiga of Poland (c. 1373–1399)
❑Jane Pierce (1806–1863)
❑Johanna Spyri (1827–1901)
❑Joséphine de Beauharnais (1763–1814)
❑Juana Inés de la Cruz (1651–1695)
❑Julia Avita Mamaea (180–235 AD)
❑Julia Cornelai Salonina (???–268 AD)
❑Julia Domna (170–217 AD)
❑Julia Drusilla (16–38 AD)
❑Julia Grant (1826–1902)
❑Julia Maesa (165–226 AD)
❑Julia Paula (???–??? AD)
❑Julia Soaemias (180–222 AD)
❑Julia the Elder (39 BC – 14 AD)
❑Julia Tyler (1820–1889)
❑Juliana Louise Emma Marie Wilhelmina (1909–2004)
❑Justa Grata Honoria (???–??? AD)
❑Kateryna Vasylivna Bilokur (1900–1961)
❑Kathe Kollwitz (1867–1945)
❑Kerstin Anita Marianne Ekberg (1931–)
❑Kim Jung–Suk (1917–1949)
❑Kristina Augusta, later Christina Alexandra (1626–1689)
❑Kyneska of Sparta (c. 440 BC–???)
❑Laskarina Bouboulina (1771–1825)
❑Letitia Tyler (1790–1842)
❑Letizia Ortiz Rocasolano (1972–)
❑Licinia Eudoxia (422–462 AD)
❑Livia Drusilla (58 BC–29 AD)
❑Lou Hoover (1874–1944)
❑Louisa Adams (1775–1852)
❑Louise Henrietta of Nassau–Oranien (1627–1667)
❑Lucretia Garfield (1832–1918)
❑Lucy Hayes (1831–1889)
❑Ludovica Margaretha von Lothringen (???–1631)
❑Lyudmila Todorova Zhivkova (1942–1981)
❑Madame She Ziang
❑Madame Zian
❑Magdalena Sibylle of Saxe–Weissenfels (1648–1681)
❑Magnia Urbica (???–??? AD)
❑Maha Chakri Sirindhorn (1955–)
❑Manlia Scantilla (???–193 AD)
❑Marcia Euphemia (???–??? AD)
❑Margaret Taylor (1788–1852)
❑Margaret Thatcher (1925–2103)
❑Margaret Theresa of Spain (1651–1673)
❑Margrethe II of Denmark (1940–)
❑Maria Amalia Josefa Anna of Austria (1701–1756)
❑Maria Amalia of Courland (1653–1711)
❑Maria Anna Elisa Bonaparte Baciocchi Levoy (????–1820)
❑Maria Anna Sophia of Saxony (1728–1797)
❑Maria Antonia (Theresia Josefa) of Austria (1669–1692)
❑Maria Carolina of Austria (1752–1814)
❑Maria Cebotari (1910–1949)
❑María Corazón Sumulong “Cory” Cojuangco Aquino (1933–2009)
❑Maria Eleonora of Brandenburg (1599–1655)
❑Maria Elisabeth of Austria (1680–1741)
❑Maria Ernestine Franziska (1687–1758)
❑Maria Gonzaga (1609–1660)
❑Maria Hedwig of Hesse–Darmstadt (1647–1680)
❑Maria I of Portugal (1734–1816)
❑Maria II of Portugal (1819–1853)
❑Maria Jeanne Baptiste of Savoy–Nemours (1644–1724)
❑Maria Konopnicka (1842–1910)
❑Maria Luisa of Spain (1782–1824)
❑Maria of Romania (1900–1961)
❑Maria Theresa Walburga Amalia Christina of Austria (1717–1780)
❑Maria Theresia Henriette Dorothee of Austria–Este (1849–1919)
❑Maria Wodzinska (1819–1896)
❑Mariana of Austria (1634–1696)
❑Marie Antoinette of Austria (1755–1793)
❑Marie Charlotte de la Trémoille (1632–1682)
❑Marie Curie (1867–1934)
❑Marie de Rabutin–Chantal (1626–1696)
❑Marie Elisabeth of Brunswick–Wolfenbüttel (1638–1687)
❑Marie Louise (1791–1847)
❑Marie Noel Belizaire (????–1924)
❑Marie of Prussia (1825–1889)
❑Marie–Jeanne Lamartiniére (????–early 1800s)
❑Marilyn Monroe (1926–1962)
❑Marion Dönhoff (1909–2002)
❑Marlene Dietrich (1901–1992)
❑Martha Washington (1731–1802)
❑Martina Navratilova (1956–)
❑Mary II of England (1662–1694)
❑Mary Magdalene
❑Mary Read (c. 1690–1721)
❑Mary Todd Lincoln (1818–1882)
❑Mary, mother of Jesus
❑Masako of Japan (1963–)
❑Matylda Getter (1870–1968)
❑Melchora Aquino de Ramos (1812–1919)
❑Milonia Caesonia (??–41 AD)
❑Minna Canth (1844–1897)
❑Mirabal Sisters
❑Miriam Makeba “Mama Africa” (1932–2008)
❑Mother Teresa (1910–1997)
❑Musa of Parthia
❑Nancy Reagan (1921–)
❑Nativity scene
❑Octavia the Younger (69–11 BC)
❑Olga Nikolaevna (1822–1892)
❑Olga of Kiev (c. 890–969)
❑Otacilia Severa (???–??? AD)
❑Patricia Nixon (1912–1993)
❑Popmeia Plotina (c. 80–c. 121 AD)
❑Poppaea Sabina (30–65 AD)
❑Alexandra, Princess of Hanover and Cumberland (1882–1863)
❑Amélie, Princess of Orléans (1865–1951)
❑Anne–Marie, Princess (1946–)
❑Caroline Reuss of Greiz (1884–1905)
❑Charlene, Princess (1978–)
❑Chen Wen, Princess (577–605)
❑Diana, Princess of Wales (1961–1997)
❑Friederike Luise, Princess of Prussia (1714–1784)
❑Henriette Adelaide, Princess of Savoy (1636–1676)
❑Louise Eleonore, Princess of Hohenlohe–Langenburg (1763–1837)
❑Louise, Princess of Prussia (1838–1923)
❑Marie, Princess of Baden (1865–1939)
❑Viktoria Luise Adelheid Mathilde Charlotte, Princess of Prussia (1892–1980)
❑Publia Fulvia Plautilla (c. 185–212 AD)
❑Anne, Queen of England (1665–1714)
❑Astrid Sofia Lovisa Thyra, Queen of Sweden (1905–1935)
❑Boudicca, Queen
❑Elizabeth I, Queen of England (1533–1603)
❑Elizabeth II, Queen of Great Britain (1926–)
❑Isabella I, Queen of Spain (and King Ferdinand and Christopher Columbus)
❑Isabella I, Queen of Spain (1451–1504)
❑Joanna, Queen (1479–1555)
❑Mary, Queen of Great Britain, and Duchess of York
❑Mary I, Queen of England (1516–1558)
❑Nefertiti, Queen of Egypt (c. 1370–c. 1330 BC)
❑Queen of Sheba
❑Paola, Queen of Belgium (1937–)
❑Sofía, Queen of Spain (1938–)
❑Victoria, Queen (1819–1901)
❑Rania Al Abdullah (1970–)
❑Romy Schneider (1938–1982)
❑Rosa Luxemburg (1871–1919)
❑Rosalyn Carter (1927–)
❑Russian Royal Family
❑Sacagawea (1788–1812)
❑Salonina Matidia (68–119 AD)
❑Sālote Mafile'o Pilolevu Tupou III (1900–1965)
❑Sarah Ferguson (1959–)
❑Sarah Polk (1803–1891)
❑Sarah, wife of Abraham
❑Seia Herennia Sallustia Barbia Orbiana (c. 209–c. 235 AD)
❑Silvia Renate Sommerlath of Sweden (1943–)
❑Sirikit (1932–)
❑Sister Mary Helen MacKillop (1842–1909)
❑Slava Raškaj (1877–1906)
❑Solomiya Krushelnytska (1872–1952)
❑Sonja of Norway (1937–)
❑Soong Ching–ling (1893–1981)
❑Sophia Alekseyevna of Russia (1657–1704)
❑Sophia Loren (1934–)
❑Sophia of Hanover (1630–1714)
❑Sophia of Nassau (1836–1913)
❑Sophie Helen (1965–)
❑Sophie of Brandenburg (1568–1622)
❑Sophie, Duchess of Hohenberg (1868–1914)
❑Srinagarindra (1900–1995)
❑St. Anne
❑St. Barbara (third century)
❑St. Catherine of Alexandria (287–305 AD)
❑St. Elizabeth of Hungary (1207–1231)
❑St. Helena of Constantinople (c. 250–c. 330 AD)
❑St. Hildegard of Bingen (1098–1179)
❑St. Mary
❑St. Matilda of Ringelheim (c. 895–968)
❑St. Sofia the Martyr (???–137 AD)
❑Statilia Messalina (35–68 AD)
❑Steffi Graf (1969–)
❑Sulpicia Dryantilla (???–260 AD)
❑Susan B. Anthony (1820–1906)
❑Teresa de Francisci (1898–1990)
❑Tiye of Eqypt
❑Ulpia Marciana (48–c.114 AD)
❑Ulpia Severina (???–after 275 AD)
❑Ulrika Eleanora (1688–1741)
❑Umm Kulthum (c. 1900 – 1975)
❑Valentina Vladimirovna Tereshkova (1937–)
❑Valeria Messalina (17 or 20 – 48 AD)
❑Vibia Sabina (83–c. 137 AD)
❑Victoria Ingrid Alice Désirée, Crown Princess of Sweden (1977-)
❑Virginia Dare (1587–????)
❑Wang Zhaojun (c. 50 BC–??)
❑Wilhelmina I of the Netherlands (1890–1948)
❑Wu Zetian (624–705)
❑Xenia of St. Petersburg (c. 1719–c. 1803)
❑Yasmine Pahlavi (1968–)
❑Zenobia of Palmyra (240–c. 275 AD)
❑Zofia Kossak–Szczucka (1889–1968)